NAPIER UNIVERSITY LIBRARY
3 8042 00252 5499

Turn Your Business Around!

— SUZANNE CAPLAN —

PRENTICE HALL
Englewood Cliffs, New Jersey 07632

Prentice Hall International (UK) Limited, *London*
Prentice Hall of Australia Pty. Limited, *Sydney*
Prentice Hall Canada, Inc., *Toronto*
Prentice Hall Hispanoamericana, *S.A., Mexico*
Prentice Hall of India Private Limited, *New Delhi*
Prentice Hall of Japan, Inc., *Tokyo*
Simon & Schuster Asia Pte. Ltd., *Singapore*
Editora Prentice Hall do Brasil, Ltda., *Rio de Janeiro*

10 9 8 7 6 5 4 3 2 1

Library of Congress Cataloging-in-Publication Data

Caplan, Suzanne.
Turn your business around : hands-on strategy for long-term survival / Suzanne Caplan.
p. cm.
Includes bibliogragphical references and index.
ISBN 0-13-302068-1
1. Corporate turnarounds--Management. 2. Small business--Management. I. Title.
HD58.8.C33 1994
658.4'063--dc20 94-31962
CIP

ISBN 0-13-302068-1

Prentice Hall
Career & Personal Development
Englewood Cliffs, NJ 07632
Simon & Schuster, A Paramount Communications Company

Printed in the United States of America

To Vera.
To teach is also to learn.

Acknowledgments

I could never have written this book, managed my practice, and continued my activities without the organizational skills of Sherry Truesdell. She maintains my database and my sanity, and I value her work. The other half of my team is Laurie Harper—agent, advisor, and friend—who not only attends the birth of a project but takes responsibility for its upbringing as well. My personal and professional gratitude is beyond the realm of mere articulation.

I have worked with a number of courageous entrepreneurs who triumphed over adversity—Bob Erikson and Karen Underhill come immediately to mind. And I have enjoyed a team of managers who moved forward with an inspiring combination of committed purpose and great broken field running—Dennis Pappalard, Andy Laser, and Tom Cunningham.

My advisors continue to be the professionals who exemplify the true sense of the word—always interested in the welfare of clients and customers. Tom Nunnally is a banker any entrepreneur would be fortunate to work with, and Don Phillips is a lawyer I would always welcome on my side. Mary Bower, another attorney with integrity and a great empathy for clients, is always a valuable resource.

My friends and personal advisors include a charming cast of characters—Jean Hunter, Paul Mason, Norm Belt, Johnie Champ, Sam Mullen, Jeff Cowan, Jane Rectenwald, Mark Bibro, Mike Reilly, Debbie Phillips, Stephanie Schrass, and Barbara Davis. And a special thanks to Vera Auretto whose profound insights about herself and others were a source of inspiration to me as well.

Preface

If you are concerned that your business has gone through a downward cycle and you're not sure how to turn it around, this book is for you. The journey back can be a complicated trip and this book will give you a road map to develop a strategy that will work for your company, starting with some emergency steps to take once you start the process. It is also a reminder that no matter how caught up you are in the day-to-day struggle, you must be attentive to your ongoing business operation. Your customers and your employees require encouragement and motivation from you to continue to provide a vibrant business environment for the company to return to health. After all, a business is a living entity, and you don't want the surgery to be a success only to have the patient die.

This is a four-part program that consists of the following:

- How to take the fast action that will stabilize your current operations.
- How to take an analytical view of your entire operation to determine where the problems are.
- How to implement the corrective measures necessary to return the business to profitability.
- How to move forward toward a more secure future.

The first thing you have to do is stabilize your operation. Treat the most immediate concerns that have probably become very distracting. You need to be able to concentrate on moving forward to solutions rather than being consumed by the day-to-day crises that may have taken over your workdays.

The second step is to stand back and take a cold, hard look at your operation. Analyze what has worked well, and face the aspects of your operation that are performing poorly. If you can't be totally objective, find someone who can, someone you trust, and someone you will listen to.

Step 3 is taking corrective measures—some of them may be painful. Cutting personnel, selling off inventory or equipment, and perhaps moving to a smaller, less costly location are some of the difficult decisions you may have to make.

Finally, your last step is the one you take forward to recovery. It starts with finishing the implementation of the recovery plan you've created and ends with the satisfaction of a second chance. Restarting your business can be as creative as beginning it the first time—not a sign of failure, but a sign of success. Change is the order of the day, and this proves that you are able to forge new ground.

My first book, *Saving Your Business* (Prentice Hall, 1992), was about successfully negotiating through Chapter 11 bankruptcy, and I know that even when a company deteriorates to that level, there is still a chance to restructure and revive the business. But it is a lot easier to accomplish if the control remains with the owner and isn't shared by the court, as it is in a bankruptcy. The sooner you face the reality of your current business circumstances, the better your chance will be to grasp the reins before someone else gets control.

If you are reading this book because you have a nagging feeling that everything isn't going right, congratulations!

In addition to the four-step program, there is a complete case study showing how the theory works in practice. We have also included answers to the most frequently asked questions of accountants, attorneys, bankers and consultants who work with turnaround situations. The book is a comprehensive program meant to guide a business back to the right track.

Contents

Introduction

For a new entrepreneur in the early stages of growth, challenge, and successes, big and small, the days are not long enough. For the owner of a mature company facing economic downturns, market disruptions, personnel problems, or financial distress, the days are too long and the nights are endless. It's a feeling I can understand—in 21 years of running a business, I've been there a few times. The first time can be a real terror, and it's hard to know where to turn.

Currently, my consulting practice is focused on turning around small companies—some needing major overhauls, some minor adjustments—and my days are regularly spent with entrepreneurs in crisis. Some are worse than others, but I have found very few that are hopeless. That is fact, not just wishful thinking.

One of my clients who has made extraordinary progress over the past year was in real panic when he found me. Over lunch, Barry confided that he was sure that his company was bankrupt (since I had just completed a book on the subject, I was being asked for sage advice on how to survive the experience). I refused any and all comment until I had completed a review of his financial statements, had looked at his industrial supply business in person, and had met with his managers. My conclusion was that while the company had uncomfortable cash flow problems (sales that had been hovering at the $3 million mark had dropped by almost 15 percent), the business was not insolvent and therefore not technically bankrupt. Convincing Barry of this fact was not easy, but he decided to go along with my theory. Together we developed a plan for survival and recovery. With a few bumps and mistakes along the way, it began to work, and while sales have not bounced back the way any of us would like, the company is stable and Barry is once again energized by the future prospects. My experience with this business formed part of the basis for conceiving this book. I have since worked with other companies with equal success.

Most of us who choose to fly solo are optimists at heart, and our spirit may carry us through the early days of any difficulty. We may not have really expected or planned for the tough times, but we remain assured that they will pass. That was usually the case in the past. Current times have altered that reality, and you may be in the middle of a serious change.

THREE QUESTIONS TO ASK

There are several critical issues to consider and the sooner you ask yourself some tough questions, the better.

1. How Low Will It Get?

Recessions are uneven affairs, particularly recent ones—some sectors and some areas get hit harder than others. Are your experiencing flat growth, or are your revenues in a deep decline? Is the demand for your product or service just soft, or is it diminishing permanently? You may have to face substantial restructuring just to survive.

2. How Long Will It Last?

Even if your industry is only in a temporary contraction, it may feel like free fall, but it will eventually find its own bottom and land. However, declines as steep as 30 percent may happen in as little as six months. During the 1992 Gulf War, revenues of restaurants and other entertainment businesses dropped precipitously as most consumers chose to stay home glued to their TVs. But once the war ended, business began to recover.

On the other hand, a number of entire industries are permanently contracting, such as steel and defense-related industries, and when the initial drop is over, there will be little or no new growth. Be realistic about deciding where your business is now and where it will be heading over the next few years.

In the flat-growth economy expected for many sectors of American business for the next few years, there won't be any steep decline to alert you, just a steady, unforgiving lack of forward progress. The condition is insidious and easy to ignore, yet just as dangerous as a serious recession.

3. Do You Have a Plan for Survival?

If you have been in business for a while, you probably operate your company more from instinct than from a predetermined plan. Most small business advisors stress the need for a written document (the much touted business plan), but for most of us, our day-to-day tasks take all the time we have, and anyhow, we would probably deviate more often than stick to the plan.

When your own company gets into difficulty, however, it does become *absolutely critical* that you take the time and make an honest assessment of the current situation. Determine the steps you are going to take to stabilize your operation and turn it around, and then commit them to writing. It is a mistake to think you can dance your way back to prosperity. And the longer you take to face this realization, the less likely your business is to survive. It's that important!

CHANGE IS ALWAYS A CHALLENGE

Business conditions in the 1990s have not been very friendly to many differing small companies. Change has come quickly to many industries, and there has been little vibrancy in either the consumer or industrial markets. The factors causing these conditions are numerous: some are domestic, such as the accelerated spending binges of the 1980s and the resulting tightening of credit in the 1990s as well as the cut in defense spending; some are global, such as increased competition from emerging nations and the difficulty in Europe with its unifying into one free economy while simultaneously absorbing the Eastern bloc nations. Whatever the cause, the result is clear. Business is tougher than ever.

More companies are fighting over the same market to create a semblance of growth. The competition usually is waged over pricing, and the individual consumer and the industrial buyer now expect discounts and are unwilling to accept higher prices. The resulting pressure is on profits, and no small business can stay in business very long without profits. You can borrow some money to carry you through a temporary time of loss but if you don't get back into the black, there is little chance you will be able to pay it back.

Contrary to the claims of many bankers, the 1990s have been a time of tight money, and it may be hard to borrow as much as you need, want, or even deserve. After the banking scandals of the 1980s, most commercial banks returned to their conservative roots. You can't get a loan unless you can prove that you don't need it—not an easy task for an entrepreneur about to have an anxiety attack. Interest rates may remain low, but how does that help if you can't get the financing your company requires to expand and meet competition?

If you started your business in an expanding economy or in the midst of growth in your market, the initial go-round in a downturn may be very disconcerting. The first thing you notice is that it isn't any fun anymore, and your personal stress may grow with the severity and duration of your problems. Don't let it paralyze you; the stakes are high and your leadership is crucial. Grab control of the reins and point yourself in the direction of a turnaround. It may be a rough ride, but the desire and skills that brought you into this game of entrepreneurship can make you a winner again.

PART ONE

Acute Care

What to Do First

CHAPTER 1

Cash Is Your Life Blood—Store Some

Most business owners understand the difference between cash flow and profits and know that both are required for long-term success. Eroding profits may take a long time to cause a problem for a company, but a sudden decrease in cash flow will cause immediate discomfort. On the other hand, sufficient cash flow may unfortunately mask potentially serious distress.

The airline industry is a good example—they can and do lose hundreds of millions of dollars each year, but because of their continued high cash flow, the companies stay afloat. As long as there is cash to pay the most pressing bills, most creditors can be kept at bay.

Whenever a serious downturn occurs in any sector of the economy, small business feels it first and often experiences greater difficulties than larger corporations. A sudden drop in cash is a nightmare to most entrepreneurs.

It is only logical, therefore, to create a cash cushion as the first step of any turnaround. You need to do it for solid business reasons as well as personal ones. From the perspective of your company, if you have funds available, you can make at least partial payments to satisfy vendors, an upcoming payroll won't keep you worrying for days, or your bank won't get wind of your problems and take actions to make them worse.

From your personal perspective, your business situation can create stress in your life that may be overwhelming at times, and having the cash to deal with at least some of the issues will make things easier for you. It's almost impossible to have a clear head to make decisions and exercise strong leadership if you have to spend your time selling personal assets or borrowing from friends to pay employees or vendors who are threatening to shut you off. If you reduce this immediate roadblock, your time can be spent on critical analysis and keeping the ship afloat to sail again.

SIX STEPS TO CREATE INCREASED CASH FLOW

The following six steps create increased cash flow:

1. Increase collection activity.
2. Solicit advances on big jobs.
3. Slow down payables.
4. Draw on credit lines.
5. Sell excess inventory.
6. Decrease expenses using barter instead of cash payments.

Create Cash Flow by Diligently Collecting Receivables

Many small business owners are the chief salesperson of the operation and have developed personal relationships with their customers. These friendships can make the owner less likely to enforce tough collection policies. If this is the way your company operates, you probably do little of the collection calling yourself, but it is absolutely necessary that you assign the task to someone in your organization; you make sure that it is being done regularly and require that reports be given to you. If this isn't the case currently, get your bookkeeper or controller on the job immediately.

If you are in a cash crunch, it may also be true for your customers, but that doesn't mean they shouldn't be gently reminded about what they owe. If no one ever asks, you may never get paid, and that could be disastrous for your business. What may be required is a friendly call from you to bring at least a partial payment, and these may be the critical dollars at this time.

You should develop procedures that become automatic once they are in place. At the end of each month, statements should be sent to all customers showing their outstanding balance. When a bill becomes 45 days old, a friendly written reminder is appropriate. After 60 days, a call is in order, and after 90 days, real action should be instituted. I know that there are concerns about losing a customer, but you really must ask yourself if you want the ones that don't pay their bills. Why not just give them product or service for free and save the administrative cost?

Offering discount terms may speed up cash flow. Although a 1 percent discount will affect your bottom line, this may be a viable short-term program to ease the financial squeeze. If profits have been the ongoing problem for your business, you need to be careful about which one of your customers you offer this program to and how long you keep it in effect. You may find that you have some customers who take the 1 percent and still don't pay in the five- or ten-day period you require. If this happens, bill them for the unearned discount and cancel the program.

ESTABLISH A SUCCESSFUL COLLECTION PROGRAM A good collection program involves the following:

- Check references before granting credit.
- Always establish terms in writing with customer.
- Send regular statements.
- Make calls on past due accounts.
- Be prepared to take action (legal) on customers who won't pay.

Ask for a Down Payment on a Big Order

When I was in the midst of restructuring my manufacturing business, the toughest money crunch came from a big order, something I wanted and dreaded at the same time. With limited cash, the purchase of inventory and weeks of pay required to complete the work could literally drain us dry. Then, the watch for payment began, and at times, a check arrived hours before an unfunded payday. It's a tough way to live.

I once shared this dilemma with a good customer and asked if there was some incentive I could give to secure a partial payment up front. We agreed on a discount, and I billed 50 percent of the order in advance. Then when we shipped, I billed the balance. This deal released my other cash for ongoing expense and really helped my company. I would not have suggested it to many of my customers, and you must have a track record with any customer you approach.

One of my clients is a contractor who has suffered severe losses doing subcontracting work for very large jobs. On several occasions, the jobs came to an end and he wasn't paid in full. This caused serious cash flow problems and threatened his entire operation. While we worked on reorganizing his entire financial structure, he had serious need for cash to fund his operation. We approached several of his large customers who had long-term working relationships with his company and asked for upfront payments to ease our problem. This was not usual procedure in the industry, but our request was met as a helpful accommodation and our customers funded our recovery.

Slow Down or Renegotiate Your Own Payables

The goal of this program is to hold on to cash as long as possible, so you'll want to take extra time to pay your own bills. Start by delaying payments 10 to 15 days, and that may be a sufficient cushion, particularly if your own receivables come in at an accelerated pace. Some vendors may not call, but don't use that as an excuse to avoid making any payments at all. You don't want to get noticed as a deadbeat because once your vendors realize how delinquent you are, they may decide to take strong action and begin to require cash in advance, which will defeat the whole program.

If you can't pay a bill in full, offer to make a partial payment. Your creditor may not be happy, but having some cash will encourage them to accept most reasonable offers. You may even try to work out a long-term payout on current bills and then pay promptly for new invoices. This will help you hold on to cash; your vendor eventually gets paid in full and keeps a good customer who is experiencing temporary difficulty.

Whatever strategy you decide on, you should always communicate with a creditor. Not taking or returning phone calls is a great mistake that can escalate a late payment into a collection action or perhaps even a legal action. If you let your vendors know what's going on and when they can expect at least some payment, they are less likely to turn the account over to someone who will charge to collect it. Always communicate, and if you have been sitting on your cash, you should be able to make at least a partial payment.

Everyone understands tough times—no one wants to lose all their money on a customer.

NEVER "BORROW" MONEY FROM THE IRS As you are slowing down payables, you may also be considering making your tax payments a bit late. After all, you've done it a few times accidentally and no one even noticed. My unequivocal advice to you is *don't.* If you are short on payday, delay payroll for a few days for all or at least some of your employees. They won't like it, but it is far less risky than making the net payroll and not depositing tax funds.

You may not hear from the Internal Revenue for weeks, or even months, about a missed withholding deposit, but when you do hear, you will be shocked by the penalties and interest that can be added. There are 25 percent initial penalties on failure to file and failure to remit and then interest on top of that. The tax due can double in no time. Bankruptcy lawyers report that over 40 percent of their clients are driven into court over tax problems. It is a slippery slope—don't take the first step off the edge.

I have worked with a number of clients who fell into this dark hole, and I have seen demand letters for hundreds of thousands of dollars. Owing the IRS money is not an easy problem to solve. While the government may accept a payment plan, it is just as likely to demand all the money due in 30 days, and it may go in and take it from your account by levy.

If you have already developed this problem, the worst thing you can do is ignore it or try to avoid facing it. If this is the first time it's happened to you, there is a real possibility of agreeing to a plan to settle your account. See an attorney immediately, and have him or her start negotiating with the IRS before any enforcement action begins.

Draw on Lines of Credit

A good banker is an excellent resource for a small business owner, and it is a relationship that should be cultivated carefully. Always be truthful with your banker, not only to enhance your credibility but because you never know what help they may be able to give you during difficult times. Every knowledgeable banker knows that businesses go through cycles, and they won't be shocked if you tell them things are a bit tough.

Any written document you turn in to the bank must be accurate, and it is never good policy to misrepresent the condition of your business. In some circumstances, to do so might constitute a fraud.

However, if your company has been granted a line of credit, there is no reason not to draw on it during tough times. Even if your account is up for review and your line may be reduced, it is yours now. It might be a good idea to draw down the line and park the money somewhere. Even if your credit line is reduced, few banks will demand immediate payback, and the cash will be available for an emergency. If you pay a little back from time to time, you may not even get their attention.

Open a Second Bank Account

There is nothing illegal about parking money from bank A in a new account with bank B, and now may be the right time for that new business account. The money should not be in your personal account. It is not always easy to predict how your banker will react if your business doesn't begin to turn around and you need additional forbearance or even more capital. Some banks can be very accommodating to customers, especially if they are long-term clients. But your particular branch manager may have just been burned by a loan gone sour and want yours off his desk so he won't get noticed by top management that way again. Loan losses are an important form of evaluation for bankers, and there are those who would rather take *no* risks so that they show *no* losses. It may have little to do with you or your business. Try not to take it personally.

A second banker may have a different attitude and show a real interest in developing you as a new customer. This banker may be willing to be more liberal in loans and more competitive in rates. Banks become aggressive from time to time in developing new accounts and placing new loans. After all, interest from loans is a major source of bank income, so holding cash usually makes little sense. A new banking relationship may be just what your company needs.

Identify and Sell Dead Inventory and Unneeded Equipment

The early stages of a business turnaround is *not* the time to liquidate usable but slow-moving inventory at below what it actually cost. If you know the merchandise will eventually sell at a profit, try to hang on to it. Selling out everything in a panic for cash is a form of internal liquidation that will only serve to increase your losses and jeopardize your future. Control the impulse. You want to have a business left worth saving.

On the other hand, if you have products you will never sell or equipment you will never need, now is the time to turn them into cold hard cash regardless of the discount. Money in your bank account is more valuable to you than obsolete inventory on your shelf or equipment that has to be stored and insured.

Call in an auctioneer or even a surplus buyer. There are a number of them in every city listed in your phone book and also a large number of national dealers. If you have an extensive amount of inventory, try dealers in other parts of the country. A good source nationally is a paper called the *Closeout News,* located in Holland, Michigan, at (616) 392-9687. The paper includes almost a hundred pages of ads from surplus liquidators. A review of this paper will give you the chance to see who might be likely to specialize in your type of inventory as well as what prices your excess inventory might bring. Always seek multiple offers and don't be shocked if you are offered 10 or 20 percent of the actual cost. Accept the best offer you can find, bank the money, and don't look back. Your whole focus is to stabilize your business enough to have the chance to move forward. Put the cash to good use, and it will serve its purpose.

Barter for Goods Instead of Buying Them

Every strategy in this chapter is meant to increase the amount of cash you will have to ease your way through current difficult times. You may also need to finance new opportunities for the future. This exercise is all about building cash reserve and holding on to that cash. Eventually you will look at a number of ways to make long-term cuts in cash expenses, but in the meantime, consider whether there may be goods or services that you manufacture or provide that can be used to trade for goods and services that you need. This is known as barter.

You can join a formal barter group, but many of them require a fee up front to register your company. Joining one may not make sense if you'll be trading on a limited basis. What you can do is start your own program by approaching a vendor who is also a customer and see if you can trade goods or services on a more or less equal basis. Keep track of the transactions you are exchanging, and don't let them get out of balance. You don't want to be hit with a bill for cash out of the blue.

Several of my clients use this system very effectively. I have seen it most often with the media, particularly radio stations. They will trade on-air advertising time for those items they require, such as office supplies, printing, travel, and even restaurant use. It may be particularly useful for businesses that deal in perishable items such as advertising time or airline seats that, if they are not sold, are not savable for sale later. Use your imagination.

There may be sales tax implications in barter transactions as well as recording the revenue as sales for any corporate tax as well. You may want to check with your state Department of Revenue or with your accountant.

Remember, also, that simply because you are not per se paying for the goods or services of your vendor, don't use more of them than you can justify for your business need. Your long-term goal is to control costs, whether they are for cash or trade.

HOW YOUR BUSINESS AFFECTS YOUR PERSONAL LIFE

What happens to your business happens to you. The two can seldom be separated because you have benefited from your financial success, and inevitably you will suffer from any rescues. You know this because you have most likely personally guaranteed the company's loans and may feel as if the entire debt could come crashing down on you at any time.

There are several things for you to consider this early in the game:

- Conserve your own cash; you may need it.
- Don't commingle personal assets as a short-term infusion into the business.

Get Control of Your Personal Cash Needs

At the same time you are trying to store extra cash to protect your company, you should be doing the same thing personally. During the years that your business was doing well, you may have drawn a substantial salary. Now the reverse is going to be true. These could be times when you will have to make decisions between paying yourself and paying a bill. If you are personally cash short, that decision will be made even tougher.

My insurance agent told me about the time he faced a critical business situation and immediately dealt with it by cutting his own personal expense. The insurance company that had been his main carrier announced that it was no longer going to write auto policies in our state, and the loss of this revenue could have disastrous effects on his agency. Along with some strong extra effort at marketing, which minimized the impact on his revenue, one of the first things George did was cut back drastically on his personal overhead, including all memberships and purchases that were not necessary. He prepared for the struggle before it began. You should do the same.

Once you have completed your analysis of the company and developed a projection of how long it will take to turn it around and how deeply you will have to cut into the costs, you will have a better handle on any adjustments that are going to have to be made personally, but while your circumstance is still in flux, keeping yourself liquid and flexible is good advice. It is tough enough to worry about the financial condition of a business but if you are personally in jeopardy, the stress may be unbearable.

Be Cautious About Putting Personal Funds into the Business

One of my clients kept his business alive by refinancing his home and summer place and putting all the cash into the company to keep it liquid. That was a mistake in the beginning and a mistake in the end. The extra cash masked most of the real symptoms of the problems and allowed him too much time avoiding the reality of the company's situation. By the time he ran out of personal funds, the problems had become too severe to correct. At some point in the months before the business closed, he was unable to take any salary, and he was getting crushed by two large mortgages. Finally, when it was over, there was no way to pay any of it back. The company was liquidated by the secured lender, and my client had to help with the sale but received none of the proceeds.

Consider carefully all these issues before you put personal resources into your business. You may need them for yourself, and you may only buy a little time, not enough to complete the job at hand! Instead, invest human capital to redirect and reenergize the business.

Use Your Cash to Stabilize Your Business and Yourself

The goal of any turnaround is to refocus the company in the direction of new business and profit. The first task is to firm the footing underneath the existing operation, and conserving cash is a good way to begin. Now on to step 2 of immediate care.

SUMMING UP

The following is a plan to increase your available cash and ease your stress:

1. Speed up receivable collection by putting a tough program into force and keep up with it.
2. Slow down your own payables with partial payments or short-term forbearance from creditors.
3. Negotiate down payments from customers before you begin a big job.
4. Draw down lines of credit that are already in place for your business.
5. Develop a second banking relationship and see if you can negotiate better loan deals.
6. Sell excess inventory and equipment that you will not be able to use in your normal operation.
7. Use barter instead of cash; you may even develop new customers out of this system.
8. Cut back on your own draw at least temporarily and scale back personal needs to accommodate this action without increasing your own pressure.

CHAPTER 2

Pull Back All Projects for Review

One of my first major consulting projects was for a few months with a small manufacturer on what they described to me initially as the need for increased sales and marketing efforts. Once I got into the company and did some serious investigation, I realized how deep and pervasive their problems went within the organization. Most of their contracts were on razor-thin margins, and their manufacturing personnel were so undisciplined that little work was done on time and in budget.

Equipment wasn't well maintained, and there was always pressure from the same employees who neglected maintenance to replace older machines rather than fix existing equipment. A small loss was quickly turning into a hemorrhage of red ink, and everyone labored under the assumption that all they needed was one new hot-shot salesman. In the beginning, I had lobbied for a stronger marketing plan before bringing someone else on board, but I soon realized that a structural change was required. At times I had to control the impulse to stand in the middle of their building and yell, "STOP!" Finally, I got the full attention of the owner and convinced him to take control and put everything on hold until we could determine which direction was up.

FOUR CAVEATS: A QUICK FIX IS NOT THE ANSWER

A company develops over the years, and while it is doing well, everyone wants a part of the credit. When it begins to get into difficulty, no one wants to take any of the responsibility. Everyone hopes that one quick fix will solve the problem and that everyone includes the owner. But the fact is that like a car or even the human body, the first symptom of trouble is often ignored, and by the time the situation can no longer be ignored, it involves many aspects of the operation.

Even if you really believe that your trouble is localized in one or two areas, you must realize that looking for a "quick fix" is not the answer. I will caution you about the following:

1. You don't have room for even *one* more serious mistake.
2. Don't take on a new line of business just to generate revenue.
3. Hiring new employees without looking at your structure won't be a solution.
4. Now is the time to be cautious.

A Company in Distress Can't Afford Another Mistake

One of the strengths of entrepreneurship is in the energy and the willingness to create change in an organization. One of the weaknesses is the tendency to act before the issue has been completely considered. Sometimes the best thing to do is nothing. It's hard for most of us to exercise that discipline. We have always welcomed the next big challenge of developing a new product or entering a new market as a sign that we are still in the game. But the weaker your company is, the smaller the margin for error, and now you must keep that foremost in your mind.

Making a purchase of equipment that won't bring immediate return or hiring a new employee who will initially cost more than they earn could prove disastrous. Now is the time to be as conservative as you possibly can encourage yourself to be. It won't be for an extended period, just long enough to stabilize your existing operation; analyze it completely and set a new course if necessary.

As soon as you stabilize your company, your effort will be redirected to finding out what area or areas of your enterprise has brought you to this precarious situation. If you have been underpricing your products, hiring a hot new salesman will just allow you to lose more money. Buying equipment in an effort to attract new business may cost more to accomplish than the profits it will generate, and that may further weaken your cash position. And finishing an expansion that you once believed necessary may now be the opposite of what you really require. Instead of increasing your position in your current field, you may need a way to reorganize into a smaller yet profitable business. Even if you have already expended some time and cash into the project, throwing good money after bad isn't prudent. Perhaps you can carefully slow down the whole process while keeping your investment intact. The time you take now will pay future dividends.

Even if the effort to stop a change in process is enormous, my advice is still the same. The first thing you must do is get a firm grip on the operation you have been running and are very familiar and comfortable with before you change it in any way.

Don't Take on "New" Business Just to Keep Busy

I'm not recommending that your company becomes (or stays) entrenched in the status quo, because I know as well as you do that the business environment is always changing. Even if you maintain your existing business base, you should always be looking toward the future. But, if embarking on new ventures has been your weak area and your revenue has dropped, now is not the time to chase after new and unfamiliar work to find an instant fix. You may need to redefine yourself, but take time before turning everything upside down.

I worked with a small contractor who had built a successful business doing a large number of small jobs, namely, for individuals and other small businesses. He had good equipment which he was able to replace on a regular basis. Other larger contractors took note of that and began offering him a chance to bid on some big jobs as a sub. It looked like a chance to expand. Unfortunately, a number of the jobs went sour, and my client wasn't paid a substantial amount of the revenue he anticipated.

My most difficult problem in working with him was convincing him to take a hard look at what type of work he did well and could make a profit on rather than take every new job that was offered to maintain his cash flow. All "new" bids had to be carefully considered because any further losses could have completely devastated his company.

Another of my clients was a small deli restaurant that had earned a steady income until a new strip mall opened across the highway with a tenant that had a slightly fancier operation. Ben, who owned the deli, had always considered starting a catering business but hadn't pursued it beyond doing special "takeout" trays because his hours already were long and he was always looking for reliable employees.

Serious competition from the other mall shop created a 30 percent drop in sales. So Ben panicked and started his new catering service in record time. He had his first job lined up in less than two weeks. It was an absolute disaster—a Saturday evening informal dinner party that almost closed his existing business for an entire day to prepare. Only one new person was brought on board to "serve"—Ben came in early with another cook to prepare the food. By lunchtime, they still didn't have everything in hand, and most of their regular customers were neglected because there was no space left to cook individual orders. Late afternoon, in a panic, Ben closed his restaurant three hours early to finish preparation of his catering job. When the results were in, the restaurant had a $350.00 revenue shortfall, Ben had worked a 17-hour day, and if he didn't count his own time in the cost, the catering job had broken even. Not a bright beginning, and an exhausted and dejected Ben called me for help.

The fact was that catering was one of the answers for Ben, but not the first one. He couldn't afford to take on new overhead of personnel and additional equipment before he stabilized his existing operation, and he needed to study how the extra work of catering could be done without displacing his ongoing business.

A jewelry store in my neighborhood announced a big expansion into the antique business, which motivated me to stop in and see what was going on. The owner told me that over the past year his regular business had deteriorated and profits were almost gone. I asked him why he decided on antiques, and he didn't have much of an answer other than his ongoing interest in antique jewelry. Over the next few months, I seldom noticed any increased level of business at his shop until I saw the "going out of business" sale in the window, one of those "everything must go—50 percent off" type of banners.

What my local tradesman had done was increase his cost by purchasing an entire new product line and created no additional return. Now his already serious cash flow problem became fatal, and he was forced to close his store. It's a tough way to learn a lesson in patience.

YOU CAN'T AFFORD TO SELL AT A LOSS FOR LONG How often have you taken a hard look at your own balance sheet? Do you compare your net worth from one year to another? If you have been losing money for a few years, you are aware that the equity you have built up over the years has been eroding.

Cash flow is important to a business, but not if it's done at a consistent loss. Most "new" businesses have an operating loss as a part of the start-up costs even when an in-place company is merely diversifying into new markets. This is a cost you may not be able to afford at this moment, but even if you can, you want the time to think it through before heading out on a new path. If you work your way through the stabilization and analysis portion of your turnaround, your chances of success will be better and your new direction will have a better long-term implication for the success of your business.

In addition, the cash you are beginning to conserve and the funds you will create by cost cutting and possible liquidation of unnecessary goods can be used to adequately fund the new project. A well-financed launch has a better potential for a successful outcome, and you won't have to work as long to get it to that stage.

Freeze Hiring Plans

Now is not the time to take anyone new on board even if it is to replace someone who is leaving, although in the latter case, there may be some exceptions. A key slot may need to be filled and you should hire someone.

But in most cases, taking the extra time to review the operations of a department will be worthwhile. Perhaps if you did the job yourself for a few days, you would gain some insights into how it could be more efficient or even if it were a job that could be eliminated. For example, if you have one individual doing all the purchasing for your company, is it possible to allocate budget authority to a number of others for their own departments and have them make purchasing decisions? They would have a better idea of how much money is spent and may even show you ways to create savings.

As for any new employees such as the surefire "hot-shot salesman" described earlier in this chapter, they usually turn out to contribute far less than you have anticipated. There are no saviors; even major league sports teams—the New York Mets, as one example—have found it almost impossible to find a single star that will make an average group into a winner. It requires the hard work of all the members of the existing group first. Once they are up to speed, perhaps someone new will be the impetus to take it over the top. You must work on your in-place team first.

Even large corporations make the mistake of believing that regardless of their structural problems, there exists somewhere a magician who can make them all go away. General Motors fired Bob

Stempel because he couldn't cure what ailed them overnight. Eastman Kodak started down the same path—one savior would create a new vision and a return to profitability. It didn't happen—he didn't stay. These companies had a bundle to search for a magic bullet—learn from their experience. It doesn't exist.

DON'T SEND OUT DISTRESS SIGNALS— CREATE A POSITIVE SPIN

Whatever project you stop or job slot you leave unfilled, do so with a positive explanation. There are a number of ways to give the appearance of stability rather than panic.

1. Slow down any projects gradually.
2. Stretch out completion dates to delay acquiring any new costs.
3. Keep in touch with potential employees even if you can't make a commitment now.
4. Be open with current staff as to when purchases may be made or hiring freezes released.

The trick to this is not to cease your activity suddenly and without any justification. Don't cancel an equipment order without first making inquiry about putting the purchase on hold for a later shipment date. Explain that you are doing some additional research before you make changes in your operation.

If you have almost come to the point of hiring someone as a new employee or to replace a current person who is leaving, let your candidate know what is happening. If the hold is indefinite, say so, but if you would still have an interest in this individual at a later time, let them know that, too. They may still want to be considered when your circumstance changes, and you may save time by having a qualified individual available when the time is right. Your explanation can be as simple as the fact that you are in the middle of a reorganization of the department and want to bring someone new on board after you have refined a new job description.

Also keep your current employees informed as to why you have decided to stop hiring at the moment. Give them some tasks to do to review their current work arrangement with the understanding that forward progress will begin again after the review is complete and new plans can be created. Always talk about the future—set new goals and keep those around you informed.

There will be many new opportunities for you to set your company in motion again, but at present, you should keep actions in control and take the time to review your options.

Keep your actions positive—you're not pulling back to fade away. Rather, your role is one of the explorer, finding new ways to move forward.

SUMMING UP

Review all new projects and hold off decisions until the company is stabilized and more analyses have been done.

1. Put equipment purchases or expansion plans on hold.
2. Analyze current business lines and new opportunities before deciding where your future effort may best be directed.
3. Abandon all hiring plans except for necessary replacements.
4. Keep believing in the future of your business and plan as if there will be one.

CHAPTER

3

Cut Expenses Across the Board

The first step back from the losses that have been threatening your company's future is to stop all the red ink. One of the main reasons you put aside all new projects was to cut back on your current outlay of cash. Unless you have embarked on some sort of major expansion drive that had dramatically increased your expenses, this will not be sufficient. What will be required is a temporary across-the-board cut of all but the most necessary expense. Since this is a short-term event, you can wield a big knife. The process goes as follows:

1. Set a percentage goal for your cuts.
2. Don't spare any department.
3. Try to combine jobs to cut wages.
4. Ask your vendors for help.

DETERMINE THE AMOUNT OF SAVINGS REQUIRED

Take a look at your profit and loss statement for the past three or six months—go back long enough to get an accurate picture of what losses you have been incurring over an average month, not just a bad one. If you include a monthly depreciation figure, back it out of the statement for this purpose. Your concern now is the cash shortage you are experiencing, not the fully depreciated loss. Eventually, you will need to accomplish a sufficient amount of both revenue enhancement and cost cutting to return to profitability. For the moment, you are attempting to stabilize your cash flow so that you don't go any further into debt, and this will be accomplished by a major cutback in expenses.

Use a Cash Flow Projection

You will need to create a cash flow analysis to find out what your target savings must be. This is different from a profit and loss statement because it uses your cash income rather than sales as a revenue amount. In other words, even if your sales were $50,000, if you only collect 80 percent of those sales, your revenue is $40,000. Use a format similar to the one shown in Figure 3.1, and begin with your next month.

FIGURE 3.1

	I	Cash available (how much will be in your account the first of the month)
+	II	Collections (all receipts received)
		____________________
=		Total available cash (all money available)
–	III	Fixed monthly expense (rent, utilities, etc.)
–	IV	Variable expense (wages, material, etc.)
		____________________
=		Cash available for debt service (loans, old bills)

If your bottom-line number is a negative or less than your outstanding loan payment, this helps to form your target cut percentage. You also need to add an amount that will leave you able to make payments on old debts so that eventually creditors will be paid off in full. Plan to pay over a year if you can.

For the purpose of the example, shown in Figure 3.2, I will use rounded numbers as a guideline for your format.

FIGURE 3.2

	Cash on hand		$ 7,500
+	Collections		25,000
	Available cash		$32,500
	Fixed expense		9,000
+	Variable expense	23,000	
	Total expense		$32,000
	Available for Debt	500	
–	Loan Payment		800
–	1/12 of Old Debt	1,300	
	Shortfall	$(1,600) (or 5 percent of total expense)	

Cut across the board is 5 percent.

Make This Temporary Cut Swift and Strong

This is not the time for putting in place budgetary changes that will be in effect for the long haul. At this moment you are attempting to conserve cash to give you the breathing room you need to work on analysis and structural change. You may not have the time to go back for a second round of cuts, and it is important as well that you appear strong and decisive. After you know what the necessary amount of savings will be, add a bit for a cushion and take out your knife. Nobody will like the sacrifice, but if all employees have to tighten their belts at the same time, they can treat it as a mission, not a punishment.

DON'T SPARE ANY SACRED COWS

If you have chosen a percentage figure with a small amount of play, you must make your cuts on every line item to achieve the number you need. I have never seen a budget that doesn't have at least a few percent of waste in it, and yours most likely follows that rule. Sit down with your employees, describe the target numbers you are trying to achieve, take out the knife, and begin to make the cuts. Solicit advice on this matter because you want to have full cooperation.

Some of the line items to give the closest consideration are

1. Travel and entertainment
2. Inventory reduction (stock less)
3. Office expense (phone, postage)
4. General supplies

Start off with items under your own control (sales expense, for example, such as travel and entertainment) and volunteer to cut out all but the most necessary expense. Take the position that this is a prudent act at this time—certainly not a major sacrifice because many of your staff may feel that the costs of these items aren't justifiable. These may be the least understood costs in business. Ask for other ideas of how expenses can be reduced, and keep a running total so you know how close you are coming and what additional belt tightening is still to come.

Review all aspects of the business operation with those who are most directly involved. Can you reduce inventory? Can you save energy (and its cost)? Can you cut out some of the phone service? Don't stop at just cash savings—ask about other efficiencies as well. If you save time—you will save money.

You may have to share more about the financial realities of your company with your employees than you have in the past and it probably won't be very comfortable. But you also may be surprised at some of the valuable suggestions that individuals will make to save time or money or both. People don't mind being told about a problem if they can be part of the solution.

COMBINE JOBS TO CUT WAGES

The days of sweat shops are long over and never were desirable in the first place. On the other hand, with computerized assistance such as voice mail and word processing, there are some jobs that have become less than full time. Can some of your employees cross-train on other jobs and ultimately make it possible to reduce employment levels by one or more? The savings from that could be enough to make your business breathe easier. You won't know unless you ask.

A company in distress puts a strain on everyone associated with it, so the suggestions that involve increased work loads and possible layoffs should come from others if at all possible. When talk of the need for personnel reductions originates from you, everyone begins to think that their own job is in jeopardy. It may undermine the team spirit you're trying to inspire and that you will need to turn the company around.

What About Pay Cuts?

The first stage of a turnaround shouldn't last longer than four to six months, because if you can't stabilize your operation by then, your problems may need more major strategies such as legal reorganization. Any pay cuts that are agreed to in this first phase will only be temporary and may be enough to buy time to change direction. You know how your pay scales compare to industry and regional averages. If you are already below them, any further requests from you will probably result in employee defection, which you certainly can't afford at this time.

If your current pay is at or above average, then consider this short-term measure. Use your absolute percentage number and inform your employees in advance of why and for how long they will be getting reduced wages. There will be some grumblers among the group, but try not to let it get to you. Perhaps you can pledge to try to make restitution when circumstances change, but don't make any absolute promises. No one will really believe your intention, so it won't make the impression you want, and if you are unable to follow through at a later date, everyone will remember that fact.

Of course, if you are operating under a union contract, you can't arbitrarily go out and cut wages without bargaining for an agreement. If your relationship has been a good one and you have been open about circumstances, you may find more cooperation than you expect. If the reverse is true and you've had an adversarial relationship, perhaps the effort isn't worth it unless the situation gets completely desperate.

CUT YOUR OWN PAY AS WELL You will need to cut your own pay by a figure high enough to make a difference, but don't make a major point of it. Again, you're trying to motivate everyone to pitch in to help, not prove how this is "hurting you worse than it's hurting them." It's all relative. One company president I know made a major point of telling everyone how he cut his pay by 30 percent while he was asking them for a 10 percent cut. Since his life-style indicated an income ten times that of his average manager, the point was lost and even backfired, allowing everyone to grumble after the meeting was over. His folks immediately cut their work load by 10 percent and that defeated the purpose. Don't bring it up and it won't be discussed.

ASK YOUR VENDORS FOR THEIR COOPERATION

When GM was in the midst of losing hundreds of millions of dollars, it began a major restructuring that included asking vendors for relief. You're not GM and can't get away with any real pressure, but there's no reason not to contact vendors and ask for any cost-saving ideas they may have. Ask specifically if they might suggest new products that work as well as ones you are currently buying at a reduced price. You never know what suggestions might be made and how it could affect your bottom line.

Ask about any quantity savings if you order more and order less often. Is there a certain level of sale that will carry a prepaid freight term? Are there products in their line that are more economical than ones you are currently using and have many of the same uses? Be candid about what you need to do and frame it in the terms that rather than finding a cheaper source of supply, you would rather work with existing vendors to get the savings that you need. One of my clients found out that if he placed more business with a single material supplier, he would be able to work on a consignment basis that really helped his cash flow.

Your Landlord May Be Able to Help

Don't forget your landlord. Even though he has a contractual relationship with you, a temporary rollback of rent isn't out of the question. If you're in a desirable location, you may be greeted with silence, but if your space wouldn't likely be easily rented to another company, a temporary accommodation may be possible. You could offer to add extra rent to the final few months of the lease after your business has had a chance to turn around. It may also help to pay the rent in two payments instead of one. Also, could you perform some work in lieu of rent?

When it comes to cutting costs, you should be ruthless—this is present survival and future growth that is at stake. What you accomplish now will have its return over the next few years so rather than look at this as a retrenchment, view it as a consolidation leading to the next push forward.

CUT YOUR PERSONAL EXPENSES

Your livelihood is very dependent on the long-term survival of your business, so this same across-the-board strategy should be applied to your personal expenses. You will have to take at least a temporary cut in pay and perhaps benefits, especially those that are discretionary, such as travel and auto reimbursements. If you have been living a somewhat lavish life-style, you may find it difficult, but let me assure you that it will be harder if you put it off until you are behind in your bills. The added stress of personal bill collectors on your back can be devastating.

There are things you can do now to ease your overhead while keeping options. If you belong to a country or private club, ask to have your membership made inactive for a year (or a season). If you have been a season ticket holder to a sporting or cultural event, sell one year's tickets to someone else while maintaining your rights to the seats. Any excuse about a temporary increase in work load is believable, and the reduction in overhead cost may really come in handy. If a car lease is coming due, consider trading down or buying a small car to use until things turn around. Talk to your family and ask for their cooperation. Family vacations may have to be scaled back and spending on your house deferred. It may be a sacrifice for a while but it won't be forever.

SUMMING UP

There are a number of steps involved in an emergency cost-cutting plan and these are the ones to follow:

1. Determine your cash shortfall by analyzing your cash flow and determining how much it will take to meet debts.
2. Cut all costs, not just a few; no department should be exempted from at least a review.

3. Look at personnel costs. Can you combine work and cut back hours?
4. What about temporary pay cuts? Be careful about how you present it to workers.
5. Talk to your vendors; ask them for suggestions and let them know your goals.
6. Talk to your landlord; a good tenant is worth keeping with some short-term concessions.
7. Include your personal expenses as well; you will be cutting your own pay, and you don't want to get behind on personal debt.

CHAPTER 4

Line Up a Support Team of Friendlies

When your business was doing well, you probably longed for more quiet moments to be alone. Now, if you resemble many other business owners facing difficulty, you are spending too much time isolated with your own stress. You may not realize it, but your exile is really self-imposed, and it's caused by several factors. First, the necessary financial cutbacks you have made will cause you to socialize less where expense is involved; you may have temporarily given up golf, sporting events, or even going out to dinner. A second reason may be that you're not sure if you really want to be in the company of others. The world around you may seem as if it's still on the move while you are immobilized in one place. It's an uncomfortable feeling but totally natural under the circumstances. And, unfortunately, you may be a bit embarrassed by your situation. This feeling is undeserved, yet it is one I see frequently among my clients. People tend to be their own hardest critics.

One of the characteristics that drives us into business for ourselves is the desire to be independent, but there are times, and this is one of them, that you really need the advice of others. If you have a board (even if the stock ownership is primarily yours), convene it and discuss current circumstances. Ask members to help you develop strategies for a turnaround; that's part of their role.

There are a number of others whom you may want to include in your newly formed inner circle and to involve in your decision-making process.

- The company accountant
- A good business attorney
- A friendly banker
- Key employees
- Trusted friends and business advisors
- Consultants
- Former employees (now retired, perhaps)
- Your insurance agent

SET UP A MEETING WITH YOUR ACCOUNTANT

Small companies have very inconsistent relationships with their accountants. In some cases, all the accounting firm does is prepare statements without much comment, and in others, they are primarily tax preparers. Few small businesses can afford the ongoing participation and advice of a CPA, and few owners would take much of that advice if offered. You know what your relationship is and if it's a constructive one, your accountant may be of great help now. It is possible that the only action you'll have to take is to bring him or her up to speed on current conditions. Invite them to your place of business so that the issues you are discussing become more tangible. Talk about ways to shore up the existing business first—is there a way to generate more cash flow or profits that you haven't considered?

I worked with a restaurant that had an extremely competent CPA available, although he was only called when profits deteriorated seriously. At that point, one of his first questions was about the last menu price increase, which had been over three years. After much discussion, a new menu was printed with an across-the-board 4 percent raise. In the first month, only two customers mentioned it, but almost $60,000 was added annually to the bottom line. A good beginning to a turnaround. Needless to say, they're not all that easy.

Have Your Accountant Review Your Financial Structure

A small contracting firm I worked with only briefly had six different loans that they were paying monthly. One loan was for a line of credit for operating money, and the rest were for equipment purchases. The owner never discussed this sort of financial structure with his accountant until he began to have trouble making the payments. The first suggestion the CPA made was to consolidate all the loans and extend the payback period of one to three years to five years across the board using an SBA-guaranteed bank loan. His payments were cut by 40 percent, and the relief was immediate. I was out of a job but my client was on the right track. That was enough for me.

You and your accountant should take a hard look at your financial statement, particularly from the view of a banker or other lender. Has your deteriorating condition become evident, and are your current ratios sufficient to keep your loans and lines of credit from being called? If you had a strong equity base over the past few years, it may be some time in the future that you will have to deal with a "hard-hearted" banker.

If you have not had a working relationship with your accountant, now it may be too late to try and develop one. You don't have the luxury of time to work out communication and understanding of how you work, think, and what your goals have been. Some accountants are more analytical than others, and some are more creative. You need strategy not micromanagement. At some point you will need the services of a good accountant—begin to ask for referrals from other business associates.

HOW LAWYERS CAN BE HELPFUL DURING TOUGH TIMES

Most business owners call their company's attorney when they are angry enough to sue someone or have received some threatening communication about action being taken against them. You may not think of your lawyer as a good business resource, but that is exactly what he or she might be. As a member of the business community themselves, lawyers have a number of resources that may be of real help to a business in difficulty. They often know individuals who can liquidate inventory or equipment without making it public knowledge. They also know where some quiet investors might be. This could be a lifesaver if you are able to sell an equity share in your business to raise cash. And, of course, your attorney can help you negotiate and structure such a deal.

What may be of greater help at this time is allowing your attorney to serve as a buffer between you and any vendors or lenders that you have been unable to satisfy. This will protect you from any anger or threats and often actually has the effect of securing forbearance from your creditors. Most of us know that collection threats are primarily bark because the legal procedure to take a judgment and seize money or property can be expensive and time consuming. Using these threats on a lawyer are a waste of time and energy, so you might be surprised when the result of your attorney's participation is an offer from the other party to find a mutual settlement in amount and terms. Worth a try, don't you think? Remember, however, that you must make full disclosure to your attorney to get the proper help.

If a collection lawsuit has been filed, your time is limited in seeking legal advice. You may have a defense such as a dispute over the merchandise or the actual amount that is owed. You must file your answer in court so that you don't lose your rights. At least if you defend a collection suit, you will have time to figure out how you are going to pay off the amount not in dispute. Don't put these threatening documents in your bottom drawer and try to ignore them. They won't go away.

This is also a case where if you don't have the existing relationship with an attorney, it is difficult to find one quickly; bring them up to speed and utilize their services effectively. It may also be costly at a time when finances are one of your major concerns. However, unlike your accountant who will be required as things improve, your attorney may be needed if business conditions continue to deteriorate. You will be better off to find, hire, and get to know a good commercial lawyer now than after a collection lawsuit has been filed against you. If your business is threatened by the actions of others, the legal advice you get (and, it is hoped, follow) may be the difference between survival or extinction.

Introduce Your Lawyer to Your Accountant and Hold Regular Team Meetings

Few of us even think about introducing our professional advisors to each other, much less sitting down with them together and talking strategy. If you've had the foresight to pick good ones, now is the time to have a group heart to heart. Discuss your current situation and produce some contingency plans for the future. If you can afford it, plan to get together on a regular basis (weekly? monthly?) until the current crisis has passed and you feel less vulnerable.

Add to this group any other advisors you may have worked with and feel would have something to add. Is there a marketing consultant who would have strategy to contribute, or a turnaround expert or a retired former employee? Be creative—the more fire power you can muster—the better!

If you have never needed strong outside advisors, it still isn't too late to put together some professionals that can really be of value. First, find someone you really respect and trust—a lawyer, accountant, consultant, or business associate. A good and frequently overlooked resource is your insurance agent—he or she works with professionals frequently and should have some astute opinions about other advisors.

Then, you want to sit down and talk as candidly as you can about what you believe is the true source of your business problems. If you have fallen behind in tax payments, find a good tax attorney, and do it immediately. Don't become so fearful of taxing authorities that you avoid them. If your cost accounting system is haywire, start off with a talented accountant. Make sure that you bring professionals in to help who have real expertise in the areas you need.

After that, you want to meet with those who have been suggested to see if you feel comfortable with them. You also may want to bring two together over lunch to see how you all interact. The only downside risk is the cost of a meal, and you are bound to go away with at least some advice.

HOW YOUR BANKER CAN HELP YOU

Many bankers are sincerely interested in the well-being of their customers and are willing to go out of their way to be of assistance. It would be naive to forget that they represent the interest of the bank, and if you confide that you will be unable to pay back a loan, they must take steps to protect their interests. One small business owner I know came from a banking background, so she felt very comfortable chatting about her problems with her former colleague who was now her banker. Until he put a hold on her account against the line of credit she had outstanding. Just doing his job!

On the other hand, if you are going through the early stages of a turnaround and trying to make decisions about where the best hope for the future of your company is, call on your banker as a potential source for information. He may be able to connect you with other customers of the bank as vendors, customers, and even joint partners. The more his client base succeeds, the better it is for the banker. If your manager understands this, schedule a meeting to explore new ideas.

YOUR KEY EMPLOYEES ARE A GOOD RESOURCE

I worked with the CEO of a small distribution company for six weeks about what he felt was "the brink of bankruptcy." In the beginning, we met out of his office, and when I was finally allowed to see the business, no one was told that I was a consultant, let alone what my mission was at the company. I spent too much time trying to convince this owner that he had resources within his organization that could help us create a plan to get over a real tough spot. He had lost a large contract and was left with over $60,000 of inventory he couldn't pay for and didn't know where to sell. His major vendor was holding shipments of products he needed until this matter was settled. The company was becoming paralyzed by this situation.

Finally, after much wrangling, we called a meeting with the office manager, sales manager, and warehouseman. The CEO was surprised to know how much his employees already had determined and absolutely stunned that each one had already been thinking about a solution. The office manager suggested returning some goods for credit; the sales manager thought if they discounted products, they would be able to sell them and recover cost; and the warehouseman said the truck drivers who made deliveries would be interested in some of this inventory at a good markup over actual cost. By the end of the first session, all these ideas were implemented and within ten days, $35,000 of the burden was lifted and the rest worked out over time. That relieved the immediate pressure, but there were also long-range issues to deal with, and now there was a new team to work on problems and solutions. I met with the whole group six times before completing the assignment, and now, I see the CEO every six to eight weeks for review. He is thrilled with the new approach, and his financials prove it is working.

Your employees know much more about your business than you realize and maybe than you like, but there is no way to avoid that. They need to hear the truth from you, and you really need their feedback. I've spoken many times about the isolation of a business owner with a distressed company—withdrawing into your office behind a closed door is the worst thing you can do, professionally and personally. And it isn't a good idea to keep key managers in the dark, either; their uncertainty will affect their work and poor job performance only adds to the company's overall woes.

YOUR FRIENDS CAN BECOME INFORMAL ADVISORS

Many of us have friends and associates who are also in their own ventures, and you may occasionally get together, if only to complain about government regulations, your bankers, or perhaps your customers. Here is one more source of advice and support that you may not have considered. I don't know of one entrepreneur who hasn't gone through at least some tough times, and most are sympathetic and have learned tricks of their own to handle the problems they face. Try to meet over breakfast very informally and see if you can recruit a few of these hardy souls to form an advisory board. Get together as often as you need to and be ready to offer advice as well as ask for it. You may end up forming joint ventures or even starting new businesses together.

Ask for Their Counsel, Not Their Money

When a closely held company is short on finances, the owner will often try anything to raise the needed money privately. That includes borrowing from family and friends. I won't make a judgment about family; I will make one about friends. Don't do it.

In life, if you are blessed with good friendship, it is a rare and valuable commodity. During the difficult times, it will be your friends who will hold fast without judgments. This will provide a needed source of support. Making them an equity partner in your business puts all that at risk. Even if they offer, consider it very carefully. If your business does not turn around and you can't pay them back, you've lost something worth more than money. I've seen these deals go all the way to court and become very damaging to everyone. At a time when you can't defend yourself, you may find yourself being attacked by someone you care about. It is very demoralizing. If you are not absolutely sure of how you will return the loan, don't get involved.

A short-term small personal loan isn't a big problem, but business loans are for bankers and other formal lending institutions, not friends. They serve a different role—that of supporter. Don't risk it.

SUMMING UP

Finding good advisors is a critical first step to any successful turnaround.

1. You should work closely with your accountant for both analysis and advice.
2. You'll need a good attorney who will advise you of your rights and protect your interests.
3. Your accountant and your attorney should work as a team: introduce them to that concept.
4. Your banker may be a good source of advice if the company hasn't gotten into serious trouble.
5. Utilize the talents of your employees; they will appreciate your confidence and have much to contribute.
6. Other business associates can help; put together an informal group.
7. Family and friends are needed for personal support as well as advice, but don't borrow money from them.

CHAPTER

5

Keep the Lines of Communication Open

There comes a day when you will have to come to terms with the seriousness of the problems your company is facing. In the early stages, you become aware that current orders are slow, even inquiries are off, and cash is short more often than usual. There is no definitive diagnostic test, no X-ray to take, only mounting symptoms. There is almost never one moment of enlightenment in the early stages. Since you know the rhythm of your company, you know when something is wrong. But the optimist inside of you (and there must be a substantial dose of that just to be in business) believes that prosperity is just around the corner. Given all this as a backdrop, when do you begin to openly acknowledge your situation and with whom?

In the last chapter, I suggested that you work with your accountant and attorney as soon as you are ready to develop a strategy for a turnaround. I also strongly recommend that you include key employees in this process. Other outsiders are brought up to speed on an "as-needed" basis.

There are a number of individuals and organization representatives whom you will want to include in your ongoing communication plans. Consider all those who may be affected by what happens to your business, and plan when they will be brought on line. Some of those may be

- General employees
- Suppliers and other creditors
- Your customers
- Family and friends

TELL YOUR EMPLOYEES THE FACTS AS YOU KNOW THEM

What about the balance of your employees? Depending how seriously your current situation has deteriorated, most of them will soon learn if they don't already know that something is wrong. For those who work in the office, the signs may be irate collection calls, certified letters, or even a sheriff serving notice of a lawsuit. For those who manage inventory, it may be products no longer available to your company because of credit holds or lost credit lines. Other indications crop up all over: deferred maintenance, COD deliveries, personnel cutbacks, or even talk in the neighborhood. Other local business owners will often get angry when their bills aren't being paid, and word may get around.

If you are already aware that your employees are discussing the condition of the company, now is the time to open your own conversation with them. If you only suspect that word has spread, check it out with your managers. The optimum situation would be for all the information to originate with you because it will be accurate and positive.

What you say is important—half-truths or unrealistically rosy scenarios may come back to haunt you. Explain what led up to the current situation (e.g., the loss of a big customer, the failure of one of your products to catch on, or general economic conditions); describe as completely as you feel appropriate what you are doing to turn it around and give at least an estimate of your time line. Be honest—tough times don't end overnight, but they do end.

You want your employees to stick with you and even exert some extra effort during tough times. A well-informed employee is a motivated one, and uncertainty is likely to cause the flight of the talented people you really need to manage a successful turnaround.

One of my clients operated a health club during a very long and extremely difficult reorganization that several times looked as if it wasn't going to succeed. The owner is a charming and open man, and he may not always have felt like sharing all the ups and downs, but he believed his employees had a right to know, and that's what he did. At regular intervals, everyone got together for an open exchange, all questions were allowed, and answers were offered. A team spirit formed among this group that was at least 50 percent responsible for the ultimately successful outcome. That isn't to say that the hard work and sacrifice were easy because they weren't. But working as a group with a single goal makes it challenging and worthwhile.

What Your Employees Tell Outsiders May Be a Critical Factor in Your Comeback

From my own perspective as a customer, the problems at TWA were evident from the attitude of their employees, regardless what Carl Icahn was issuing for public consumption. Workers were angry, and passengers weren't being treated very well. The more that trend continued, the greater the likelihood that the company's troubles would mount, and they did—until the airline was in bankruptcy.

That's not what you want for your business. You need a strong customer base now more than ever, and the care and consideration your clients receive from your employees are critical to that retention. Workers who are getting less and don't know why or even those who have partial knowledge that the company is in trouble but no information from the source are not likely to give that service. These employees become so wrapped up in their own concerns that the best interest of the company is not served. Don't let this happen. You can do much to prevent it by opening up your own lines of communication with your employees.

TALK TO CREDITORS

It may not be easy, but talking to creditors has to be done. Unanswered collection calls are the quickest way to see your company fall into a legal morass that will end badly. Not all creditors are polite and cooperative. Some may actually be abusive. But whether it is the actual creditor or a collection agency, providing no information inevitably takes the action one step further into a legal process until you may end up in court or even in bankruptcy. It only takes five creditors with claims totaling a mere $5,000 to put your business into involuntary bankruptcy.

But why let it go that far? If you can't pay your bills in full, work out a plan of partial payments or extend the deadline for sending a check. The only way to do this is by talking to the human actually collecting the bill. A series of "He's in a meeting" or "Can she call you back?" will only bring suspicion, not buy time. You have to do that in person.

I was recently in a meeting with a client and their controller began going over outstanding receivables. Every time we began to discuss a company that wouldn't take any calls or return any, the conversation became very serious about what enforcement options might have to be exercised. When the controller had some contact with a principal of the business, it was usually agreed to give the additional time for an amicable solution. The fact that you continue to communicate and eventually pay off a debt may serve you well in the future if you want to get credit again.

If you are really uncomfortable about having a conversation with your creditors, perhaps you could start the dialogue with a note or short letter. One caution here is to avoid making any promises. You would be safe using a format such as the one shown in Figure 5.1.

FIGURE 5.1
SAMPLE LETTER TO SUPPLIER

September XX, 1994

Dear Mr. Supplier:

You may have noticed that recently our payments have been slower than you normally expect from our company. Our cash flow has been strained by a colder than normal winter and lower than expected sales. We are all working diligently to correct our problems and hope to be back to a better schedule soon. We will be in touch shortly to give you an update on our progress.

We appreciate our long-term business relationship and thank you in advance for your cooperation.

Sincerely,

XYZ Company

There are other benefits you may not have realized from communicating with creditors. You may reach some individuals who have real commercial savvy and may be able to suggest general business ideas. If they are vendors who primarily sell within one industry, you might even find some marketing assistance. You may be able to sell your own slow-moving inventory to someone else in your industry and at least recoup your cost. A vendor may be able to suggest whom to call. You won't know what help is available if you don't take the incoming calls and discuss your situation.

More Good Reasons to Talk to Creditors

You will want to have an impact on what is said about your company by other businesses in the area or in your industry, but you can't accomplish this from a position of silence. You need a chance to explain the circumstances of your company's current situation and then describe your strategy for changing that circumstance. Your own spin on the subject will be much more positive than one put forth by someone unfamiliar with your circumstances. People will talk—why not participate in the conversation?

Your company may not make the recovery you expect or it may take longer than you anticipated and creditors will be forced to wait an unreasonably long time before getting paid. If all they've heard is silence, it is likely strong action will be taken, including legal action. Once lawyers get involved, it adds costs and risk. Several creditors can join together (or be brought together by one attorney) to put your company into involuntary bankruptcy. A creditor is less likely to take this type of major action against someone with a recognizable name and personality. Don't be thought of as a message or a person always "in a meeting."

COMMUNICATE WITH CUSTOMERS

Your customers will also almost always find out about your difficulties, sooner or later. Their information may come gleefully from your competitors or from an awareness that your inventory is lighter than normal or you may be experiencing constant equipment failures. Sooner or later, your business situation will become common knowledge.

Should you stonewall any inquiries? My recommendation here also is against that tactic. I would suggest that instead of silence, you opt for optimistic honesty. Be candid about how difficult the current business environment has become, but be sure to inject your plans for the change and revitalization of your company. Your listener will come away feeling that they have heard the truth from someone in the know and yet assured that the situation is only temporary and that they still have a vendor to rely on.

As in the case of your creditors, you may want to put your message in the form of a letter also. In this case, your message may look something like the one shown in Figure 5.2.

FIGURE 5.2
SAMPLE LETTER TO CUSTOMERS

September XX, 1994

Dear Customer:

From time to time, business conditions become more difficult than most of us would like. There are always a number of reasons and a number of solutions as well.

We are currently going through a major restructuring meant to make our company more efficient and better able to serve your needs quickly and at competitive prices. During this transition, there may be temporary disruptions in our service or levels of supplies. If you notice any difficulty working with us, please bring it to my attention personally.

We have always appreciated your business and look forward to many years of mutual benefit.

Sincerely,

XYZ Company

You may even be able to use your troubles to your own advantage—starting with the famous "fire sale" to raise cash. Be careful that a planned inventory liquidation sale doesn't take on the look of "going out of business." If your customers begin to develop new buying habits, it won't be easy to win them back.

Don't Be Afraid to Ask Your Customers for Help

I can remember a particularly tough time for my small manufacturing company when I wasn't sure if I could finance the next order. A particularly big piece of business, though desirable from a business standpoint, meant working capital requirements that strained every available dollar. Finally, in desperation, I admitted the problem to a customer I had known personally for a long time. I volunteered that an advance payment would make a major difference, and I would be willing to offer a discount over the 1 or 2 percent traditionally given. My offer was accepted, and it not only eased my cash burden but the incentive was sufficient to encourage this customer to offer us other large contracts on the same terms. I subsequently made the same arrangement with another customer with equal success.

TALK TO FAMILY AND FRIENDS

Those who are close to you will begin to notice a change in your behavior once the grinding stress of your situation begins to take hold. To leave them in the dark about the causes of your distress is both a disservice to them and to yourself. This is another case where lack of information can cause others to come to mistaken conclusions. Also, whether or not you realize it, the advice and support of friends and family is particularly important at this time.

One of the first outward signs you may experience is sleep disturbance. I went through it and most of my clients do also. Even now, I still wake up between 4 and 4:30 in the morning, but now I use the time to write and plan my day. I've even met with clients as early as 6:00 A.M. If you've started this pattern, don't fight it—learn to live with it. Make available other time to catch up on your sleep and plan work to do if you're up through the night. My own turnaround took over three years, and I learned to leave reading material or other work on my table before I tried to go to sleep so that if I woke up, it would be right there and I could almost pretend that I had set the alarm so that I could finish my project.

The rest of your family will begin to notice your night stalking and other stress-related behaviors, and they may worry. That's a burden you don't need now. Do what you can to describe what a "business nightmare" means, and assure them (and be assured yourself) that nothing lasts forever—this will end.

It's also important that your family members cooperate financially. Everyone must curb their spending now and they have a right to know why. It's a good "life" lesson since most of us have at least one setback in our working lives, whether it is for ourselves or someone else. A child who isn't told the truth may see your denial of something he wants as punishment, which isn't the case. A child who is asked to assist may feel good about his contribution to the family's well-being. The same is true of a spouse who should be included, not protected.

Friends Are a Source of Counsel and Support

Your friends will also notice the change in your life-style. You may have canceled vacation plans or dropped a country club membership or other things along those lines. The people you normally traveled or socialized with may suspect the reasons but not know how to approach the subject. It's often a good idea to open the dialogue with those you are particularly close to. Don't wall yourself off because you are feeling a sense of failure at not being able to keep up. You can find new activities that require less expense but may prove to be more fun. And you won't become isolated, which is very important at this time.

Friends who are in business themselves may be a good source of advice on how to analyze your situation, how to expand your market, or perhaps how to find a more cooperative banker. It's almost always better to incorporate the opinions of more than one person in your decision-making process. However, there are at least two exceptions to this rule.

The first would be when you are protecting more information than you are sharing. You may be acting properly and cautiously to withhold some data from others, but keep that in mind when they come up with ideas. If they don't have all the pertinent facts, the advice is flawed although parts may be of use. Describing how the bank is making life difficult for you without also confessing that you are months behind in payments isn't fair or constructive.

The second is free but incomplete legal advice. Friends who are also attorneys may think they are doing you a favor by giving you suggestions without charging a fee. If it's out of their specialty, it probably isn't very effective, and if it's only surface advice, the dangers can outweigh the benefits. I had one client whose best friend was a partner in a major law firm. He advised his friend to take a tough and sometimes devious stand against a bank that was causing pressure on the business. When the bank officer finally became infuriated and pressed legal action, my client's friend couldn't back up his advice with a defense because his firm represented the bank, and it would have been a conflict of interest. The company ended up in liquidation. The friends are speaking but no longer socializing.

KEEP YOUR SPIRITS UP AND YOUR OUTLOOK POSITIVE

Anyone who has gone through a serious business reversal knows how gut wrenching it can be. Allowing yourself to lose contact with vendors, customers, employees, and even family and friends is a serious mistake. Keep your lines of contact open—keep a "can do" message out, and you will begin to realize the possibilities.

SUMMING UP

There are business lines of communication to keep open with voluntary and honest information. For your business relationship, you will need to talk to the following:

1. With employees, to maintain their cooperation by answering their questions and asking for assistance.
2. With vendors, to prevent unnecessary legal action and encourage them to assist you in keeping credit available.
3. With customers, to keep up their confidence in your company.

There are personal lines to maintain as well:

1. With family, to inform them of what is happening and to secure their cooperation and support.
2. With friends, for their advice, support, and continued association.

CHAPTER

6

Consider a Worst-Case Scenario

Once a business owner comes to grips with the seriousness of the deteriorating condition of his company, he may think it's too late to do anything about it. And from time to time, that is the case. However, what is truly amazing is how much you can still do to effect a turnaround at almost any point, after years of losses and neglect. I have even had clients very late in bankruptcy reorganization with 30 days remaining until a court-ordered liquidation pull together a reorganization plan and save their business.

You don't want to get that far, but you do want to think ahead and develop a plan to fall back on—plan B or even C. Your first goal is to cure a sick company, and that's where your efforts should be focused, but if it can't be done, you'll also want to consider how to protect your personal assets from any creditors. You need to understand what a formal reorganization means and how to use it if necessary to either extend the life of your business, or protect you and your business from the actions of creditors or discharge debts that can't be paid.

LEARN THE BASICS ABOUT BANKRUPTCY

A decade ago, the mere mention of the word "bankruptcy" struck fear in the hearts of most business owners. But since a number of large public companies in retailing, heavy industry, and the airline industry have successfully reorganized in Chapter 11 bankruptcy, some of the stigma has been eliminated. It is not an easy task. I know. I took a small manufacturing company through that experience in the late 1980s, and we emerged still in business in 1990. My first book, *Saving Your Business* (Prentice Hall, 1992), came out of that experience.

A large part of my consulting practice involves small companies that are experiencing difficulties that may put them on the brink of a filing, and I know from my own experience that the longer any untreated problems are allowed to fester, the less likely the business is to recover or reorganize. If you have a strong instinct that you will need to use bankruptcy to force creditors to settle debts at less than owed or to cancel a lease or contract, learn the rules now and plan well in advance.

In addition to my book, there are a number of others that describe the various bankruptcy chapters (reorganization or liquidation) and what happens to a company involved in the process. Reading one of these is an excellent idea, as is a visit with an attorney specializing in bankruptcy reorganization. I have known companies to plan as much as a year in advance to go into Chapter 11 and restructure debt, terminate leases or contracts, or even vacate union agreements, all of which can be done in a bankruptcy reorganization.

EXAMINING DIFFERENT TYPES OF BANKRUPTCY

There are a number of types of bankruptcy covered by the law including one (Chapter 12) that is primarily for farms. Chapter 13, which is called the "wage earner's plan," is occasionally used when a small business is involved and the owner (or spouse) has a separate job. All debts are restructured based on personal income. However, the bankruptcy types most often used for business are the following:

> Chapter 11: Reorganization of debt that is usually achieved by settling with creditors for less than full amount and paying over a period of time.

Chapter 7: The liquidation of a business by selling all of the assets and paying creditors out of the proceeds.

How a Chapter 11 Reorganization Can Help You

The primary type of bankruptcy used for the purpose of business reorganization is a Chapter 11. You, as "debtor in possession," would stay in charge of your business, and you would have an initial 120 days to file a plan describing how you expect to pay back your debts. You may get up to an extra 90 days by filing a request (motion) to the court. This time is meant to give you breathing space while you address the problems in your business, perhaps find new money, and ultimately work out a plan acceptable to creditors to pay back at least a portion of your debt.

While the statistics are not very encouraging—only one company in four that files for Chapter 11 emerges as a going concern—that number is growing. And when you consider how seriously damaged most of the companies are that chose that course, perhaps it is remarkable that even 25 percent come out alive. Chapter 11 reorganization is time-consuming and can be very costly. It is now possible to get the effect without going through the formal procedures. Knowing what you can force on your creditors as terms is helpful because you may be able to convince them to accept reduced or long-term payments without the formal involvement of a court.

There are several cases where a Chapter 11 is very valuable, and these are the terms you may be able to negotiate outside of the court. Here are the primary areas.

LARGE BANK DEBT—HIGH MONTHLY PAYMENT Your bank loan is secured by the assets of your company, and you must pay the bank back in full. If what you need is a longer term and lower monthly payments, a reorganization could work well for you. If you filed a plan extending a two-year loan to five years and paying in full with interest, most courts would approve, even if your bank objected. Try negotiating this directly with your bank.

TAX DEBTS AND FORCED COLLECTION The IRS can become relentless in collecting back taxes. Even if they have levied your bank account, a bankruptcy filing will release those funds. A reorganization can give you up to six years to pay back taxes. You (or your attorney) can probably make a payment agreement without filing.

VENDOR OR UNSECURED DEBT Many reorganization plans pay 25 percent of outstanding debt, and it is paid over several years. These days, most large suppliers understand this reality. You may be able to offer 50 cents on the dollar over a year or two and wipe out a large debt to suppliers. You may have your attorney make these calls if you are uncomfortable.

The Basics of Chapter 7 Bankruptcy

The other primary type of bankruptcy is a Chapter 7 liquidation. When a company no longer has any hope of reorganization, this is how it often ends up.

At this point, the entire business (which is usually but not always closed) is turned over to the court, which appoints a trustee to sell the assets and pay debts according to a prescribed formula. If all assets are pledged to the bank, the bank takes control and conducts the sale. After the secured debt is paid, the following are then paid.

ADMINISTRATIVE FEES These are primarily legal fees, and it should not surprise you to know that the more funds available, the higher these fees will become.

PRIORITY TAX CLAIMS These claims constitute the company's outstanding debt to any and all taxing authorities.

UNSECURED DEBT If there are any funds left, they are distributed on a pro rata basis to trade creditors (or others who are unsecured).

Other Options to Examine

There are other choices even for an insolvent company. You can file a Chapter 11, and then after a few months of planning a strategy, file a liquidating plan. That means that instead of a plan of reorganization, you will file documents with the court that state how your assets will be sold and how the money will be applied to retire secured debt and then any residual to unsecured debt.

The downside of a Chapter 11 is that the legal fees charged to you in advance of the filing are much higher than in a Chapter 7 and most of the fees are paid from the proceeds of the liquidation. In addition, the Chapter 11 will be directed by you and require you to continue to work. A filing of a Chapter 7 immediately gets you out of the business with the assets taken over by a trustee. If you have a new job or new project to pursue, this gets you there faster.

However, trustees do not work quickly; they have little incentive to do so. If your assets are housed in a rented building, months could go by before a sale is conducted, and all the rent will be deducted from the proceeds. The longer a trustee keeps a case going, the more his fees add up, and these too are drawn from the sale. The effect of this is to seriously diminish the amount that is applied to your debts. In addition, you know far more than a trustee about where to sell your assets for the highest return, and you will most likely achieve a better result with lower costs. The key to decision making here is your personal situation at the time and the level of individual liability you are trying to reduce.

DETERMINE WHETHER YOUR COMPANY IS SOLVENT

It is a difficult task to determine the value of a small business. As a going concern, it has the value of its profits and the intangibles such as goodwill and market share in addition to the net asset value. An orderly liquidation might bring the cost value of inventory and less than top resale value of machinery and equipment. At this point, most goodwill and other intangibles have less worth, but the name and current accounts may be salable. A forced liquidation of your assets will bring in only pennies on the dollar, and most small businesses are not solvent if forced into such a sale.

At this difficult time, you must determine the solvency of your company because it will be incorporated into your strategy. Can you sell the company as a going concern? If you did, would the sale price be sufficient to retire all outstanding secured debt? While most owners have full intention of paying trade creditors, in most cases they are unsecured debts, and you cannot be held personally liable for these debts, particularly if your company has incorporated in either a standard C corporation or subchapter S corporation. Again, we're looking at worst case scenarios and trying to protect you and your personal assets.

The second test of solvency would be a look at the value of tangible assets, including property, machinery, equipment, and inventory sold in an orderly fashion over time. Would this type of sale realize enough cash to retire debt? If it would be close, perhaps could you sell the name or accounts for an amount sufficient to satisfy creditors? If the answer is yes, you are still in the area of a solvent business.

A good test of solvency would be to draw a balance sheet of sale values of your assets and see what the net worth would be if you conducted the sale. This is shown in Figure 6.1.

FIGURE 6.1
BALANCE SHEET BASED ON LIQUIDATION OF ASSETS

Assets	
Cash	(in bank)
Accounts receivable	(only those that are collectible)
Machinery and equipment	(what you could sell them for)
Inventory	(is it all salable discount?)
	Total
Liabilities	
Loans	(current balance)
Accounts payable	(full value)
Outstanding taxes	(consider any penalties or interest)
	Total

Difference is your current equity or your exposure (if negative).

As mentioned before, few companies, large or small, can withstand a distressed liquidation. Even if your property has real value, most buyers hold back because they expect major bargains at this type of sale. There are so many stops along the way to save value that it is a real mistake to allow your business to get to this point. It's all dependent on when you come to terms with your problem and whether or not you begin to take action to turn the situation around.

A Solvent Company Can Be Sold

The problems that have brought you to your knees can be just the challenge someone else seeks. A new owner may be able to bring in fresh capital that surely will help. New equity can be an incentive for your bank to renegotiate loans, and vendors may be willing to grant more credit than you were able to get. It may not seem fair, but it does have a value to you. If you are no longer able to turn the company around, you want to get out with your own assets intact and perhaps some cash to start over again.

If you find a buyer who pays you and assumes the company debts as well, you will be free to do just that. There are several ways to set up a deal—a sale of the business intact as a going concern or just a sale of the assets. There are pros and cons to each, and this is a case where good legal and accounting advice is absolutely essential.

I would caution you on two issues. The first is accepting a payout or a consulting fee for part of the purchase price. Forget the tax implications unless they are monumental. Think about how you will feel about being almost a partner to the new buyer. What can you do if the money isn't forthcoming? If the company you are selling has been a borderline performer, your buyer will often have the same cash problems you did. Can you afford a lawyer to fight for you if you don't get paid? The worst cases end up where the new owner goes into bankruptcy owing the former owner much of the purchase price. I personally know of five of these that have happened in the past few years. They are more prevalent than you think. If you have the choice, take a little less and take it in cash.

The second issue is the signing of any agreement that requires you not to compete. You have been working in the industry or type of business you are the most familiar with, and not being able to work within the field may be more of a problem than you believe. Unless you've always wanted to go off and become a painter, don't agree to walk away from your knowledge and your business relationships without serious consideration.

You believed in your business enough to start it or take it over. Wouldn't it be nice to see it continue on? Selling it may offer that chance.

Even an Insolvent Business Can Be Sold

You may have old equipment, out-of-date inventory, and debts to the sky, but what you also have is a name, a share of your market, and other intangible assets that may be of great value to another company in the industry. Do you have a contract or a longstanding relationship with a customer that one of your competitors is just drooling over? How about finding out what that would be worth to him? Explore how the two of you could put together a deal that would get you something even for a very troubled business.

Or is there a company in an allied business that could make a success out of an expansion in your industry? One example that I am familiar with is a janitorial supply company that expanded into safety and became a real regional player by purchasing small troubled distributors and selling extra products to their existing customers, making a turnaround happen fairly quickly. They paid very little and enjoyed a substantial return.

MAKE A PLAN IN ADVANCE

The more you find yourself driven by circumstance, the worse off you will be. It is good advice when you are starting out to have a plan, good advice to update it, and good advice to create a plan to end your company or transfer it to someone else. Review what has been described in this chapter and determine where your company really is at this time. Choose a course of action; determine who will handle all the details and exactly what your time line will be. Write it all down and review it after a day or two to make sure you really are doing what is necessary and what you want to do. Then set the plan in motion.

One of my current clients has just made some serious decisions on how we will operate over the next three months. His most obvious problem is serious cash flow problems created by several large customers who have refused to pay their outstanding bills. We also want to monitor his overall profitability. Our strategy is as follows:

1. Turn delinquent unpaid receivables over to attorney for collection.
2. Contact suppliers to secure more time to pay bills.
3. Put a small amount of additional working capital into business.
4. Determine if company can make enough profit to pay debts if we are not paid.
5. Using the results and information from the first four steps, we will decide whether a Chapter 11 may be a possibility.

A GOOD ATTORNEY IS ESSENTIAL

At this point in the life of your business, you need the help of a knowledgeable business attorney, preferably one with a substantial amount of bankruptcy experience. Don't hire someone who does not come highly recommended, and don't let the attorney's fee be the deciding factor. The level of skill and the level of cooperation between you and your counsel can make an enormous difference in the outcome of your case. Almost all successful reorganizations are directed by an experienced lawyer, and even the best outcome to a liquidation requires legal expertise. In both situations, there will be opposing forces, and your lawyer must be attentive to what's happening in the case and respond effectively. I have taken on a few clients after their cases have been jeopardized by a borderline attorney, and their situation usually has deteriorated seriously and left few options. Property that could have been saved has been confiscated, and pressure is coming from all sides.

An inexperienced bankruptcy lawyer will get eaten up alive by the system, more astute opposing counsel, and often, the judges themselves. They (the judges) have little patience for cases that drag on without reason and aren't well handled. Make a thoughtful choice in the beginning. Ask someone who has been through it or go to the court and observe lawyers in action to find one who seems talented. Don't take a risk at this stage.

At this point, it all may be a bit overwhelming. First, you've been worn down by your problems, and now your choice seems to be between bad and worse. Try to keep in mind that it won't last forever and there will be new opportunities and horizons when that day comes. I know—I've been there, and I've seen others on both sides of the nightmare as well. Sometimes, the recovery is to an opportunity for better than the original business. Life does go on.

SUMMING UP

What are the steps to take when the business is seriously troubled?

1. Consider a Chapter 11 bankruptcy reorganization by learning the rules and finding good counsel.

2. Determine the solvency of the company by drawing a balance sheet based on liquidation values.
3. Sell the business as a going concern, but be cautious about how you will be paid.
4. Sell the business in pieces to your competitors or to an allied business.
5. Conduct an orderly liquidation of all assets to get top value and retire debts.

CHAPTER

7

Develop a Best-Case Scenario

You do not want to develop a siege mentality about your current crisis. Just as it is critical to face the reality about your current problems, you must also believe that the condition of your business will improve. The steps you are taking now will make this happen, and any turnaround in the general economy or your particular market will enhance your efforts. You must think about (and plan for) an optimistic future so that you will be prepared for new opportunities when they present themselves. You don't want to allow yourself to become immobilized and stay in your current crisis longer than necessary.

If this is the first time your business has become stagnant or experienced a downturn in sales, you'll need to look around for new ways to create positive energy for the thrust forward even while you are stabilizing your current operation. Here are six key points to remember.

1. Don't liquidate valuable inventory or needed equipment for cash.
2. Set new goals for your company that assumes you will make a recovery.

3. Using your new goals, create a plan meant to achieve them.
4. Communicate and sell these goals to employees, customers, and vendors.
5. Spend some time looking at future trends.
6. Keep on developing new (and better) customers.

DON'T CANNIBALIZE INVENTORY OR EQUIPMENT TO RAISE CASH

If a recession has softened the demand for your products and you are only using a portion of your capacity, don't let the unused part go to seed. Your best equipment or most marketable inventory will likely be the easiest to liquidate but may be almost the toughest to replace when you need to move forward. It may be tempting to relieve the pressure for cash by sale of valuable assets, but it is imprudent to do it without thought.

One of my clients was being denied shipments of some product lines because of credit problems, so he sold off marketable inventory below his cost in a desperate attempt to raise funds to release the needed goods. Then when business improved and he went to replace the liquidated inventory, these suppliers also denied credit. All that was left to sell was out of date and undesirable. His company never had a chance to come back. When the second set of suppliers cut him off, his company was all but dead. No way to come back.

ESTABLISH AND SET NEW GOALS

Go back to your early days in business when you were projecting how you would grow and what your sales and profits would be like in three or five years. Even if they haven't stopped falling, find a base and build new numbers from there. While you may have used double-digit growth numbers in your original plans, now is the time to be conservative. Assume a growth pattern in line with overall economic growth, and if you are developing a new product, service, or customer base, adjust your numbers on that basis.

Now you have established new numbers that are derived from your current circumstance, and these should be realistic targets to hit.

Share them with those in your organization responsible for the effort it will take to make these goals a reality. Perhaps you can make it into a contest with small prizes or plaques for those who achieve their own portions.

CREATE A PLAN TO REACH YOUR GOALS

Don't use the current downturn as an excuse not to create a plan to reach the goal of prosperity. Once you have decided how you may be able to achieve some new success, decide on a step-by-step plan to get you there. Then write them down in the form of a new business plan. How will you find the new sales that you will need to move forward? Who are the customers and how do you expect to reach them?

If you are planning on offering a new product or service, describe it fully, working out all the bugs on paper rather than by trial and error. What is the potential for this innovation and, again, how will you reach the market to introduce it?

It is very difficult to convince a small business operator to create a new business plan after he or she is already operating the business, but if you are looking for an effective way to caste your eye toward the future, you should consider this exercise. It also is a good project to undertake in the late night hours when you aren't able to sleep.

SHARE YOUR OPTIMISM FOR THE FUTURE WITH EMPLOYEES, VENDORS, AND CUSTOMERS

Having new plans on the drawing board is a good way to inspire those stressed out by current difficulties to look to the future optimistically. If you seem to be conducting a constant disaster drill, new problems may crop up that weren't even on the horizon when you began trying to turn the company around.

For example, one industrial distributor I worked with briefly became so obsessed with his excess inventory and selling it to raise cash (which *was* an important issue) that his entire sales staff focused on this issue. In the meantime, other distributors were calling on my client's customers with new products and new marketing ideas. I learned after the fact that by the time he had raised most of the money from his inventory liquidation, one of his best salesmen had quit and the entire company was demoralized. He won the battle but lost the war.

Your employees need to see the future and, as important, to feel that they will have a contribution in it. Your vendors who may be making accommodations now should feel that there will be a payoff to their efforts down the road. And your customers will be less inclined to find new vendors if they see that you will be around to continue to service their needs.

STAY AWARE OF THE TRENDS THAT WILL AFFECT YOUR COMPANY

Many entrepreneurs are real visionaries, seeing opportunities that others miss and creating entire businesses around them. Even if you haven't based your success on cutting-edge technology or new marketing opportunities, it is still dangerous to become so involved in day-to-day operations that you exclude future trends. This is true whether you are involved in a turnaround or not. And now is no exception.

What seemed futuristic only a few years ago is becoming today's reality. The way goods are produced, sold, and distributed has undergone major change, and it continues to do so. You should spend some of your time learning about and thinking about these developments. You may come across an innovation that could improve your operation enough to accelerate your turnaround. Don't stop thinking about tomorrow.

CONTINUE TO DEVELOP NEW CUSTOMERS

In the normal life of any business, old customers leave and new ones come on board. Whether you plan for it or not, it is bound to happen. When your business is in a growth phase, you will be out actively seeking new customers. Eventually, those efforts slow down, and at the time you need new customers the most—when business is tough—that is often when your effort is stopped. Don't let that happen—you need to remain active in the market.

Problem solving, particularly on the level you are in at present, is time-consuming and energy-draining work, and it's tough to be able to muster the enthusiasm to see new prospects or to motivate your sales force to do it. But if you don't forge ahead in new customer calls, your business will continue to shrink by attrition, and when everything begins to turn your way, the growth you desire will be more difficult to find. Keeping up with sales and marketing now is a valuable course of action.

And there is a side benefit to this effort—most of us are very proud of the businesses we have built regardless of the current difficulties. Having a chance to go out and tell our stories to new prospects is a reaffirmation of our achievements and can actually help to rebuild our own confidence. So go out and see new people—it's good for your business and it's good for you.

SUMMING UP

If you only plan for the worst, you may create your own reality. If you plan for the best, you'll be prepared to seize on any opportunity. The elements of a plan for the best case scenario are as follows:

1. Keep assets intact to take advantage of better opportunities.
2. Set new goals for your company that show forward progress.
3. Create a plan to meet your new goals.
4. Make sure all stakeholders (employees, vendors, and customers) understand that you are planning for the future.
5. Spend part of your time considering future trends.
6. Pursue new customers as well as new ideas.

PART TWO

What to Do Next

CHAPTER

8

Prepare a Comprehensive Financial Analysis

Your business difficulties may have been caused by a number of areas of trouble, or they may have been precipitated by a single problem. Left untreated, even a single failure will affect other aspects of your operation, and the entire company becomes involved. The best way to create a turnaround is to determine and treat the root cause first and then attend to all the ancillary symptoms. You must start by conducting a complete analysis by looking at historical financial performance charts that compare year-to-year results. These will give you an indication of where the trouble started and a clue as to how it can be corrected.

The most typical and easiest answer to most business problems is to assume that more sales will cure all that ails the company. While this is often part of the problem, it is an oversimplification of what constitutes a business success. The gross sale number is a key indication, but it is the profit generated that is used to retire debt, invest in assets, pay investors, or form a cushion that is of critical importance to survival as well as success. If you are losing money in your operation, higher sales may only afford you the opportunity to lose even more and hasten the end of your business.

In the beginning of this book, we were dealing with the issue of cash with the emphasis on staying liquid enough to meet obligations. Generating cash is a short-term solution, and if a turnaround does not occur that will refill your coffers in the form of profits, you can't survive for the long haul.

THE MAIN ISSUES OF A FINANCIAL ANALYSIS

In preparing your financial analysis, you must include the following information:

1. Compare year-to-year results.
2. See if your expenses are in line with current sales.
3. Calculate your break-even revenue.
4. Identify which items and by how much you would have to lower expenses to turn a profit with little or no growth.

If your accounting is in a computerized database already, doing this work should not be much of a problem. Many spreadsheet software packages have analysis features built in, and you just have to enter year-end data. Even if you are on a one-write or manual bookkeeping system, it is not that difficult to do a comparison chart. It is important to make sure the categories are consistent from year to year; it would affect your analysis if expenses were allocated to one account in 1991 and completely changed to another account by 1993.

Compare at Least Three Years

Your first step is to spread out three years of numbers in a side-by-side format (see Figure 8.1). This allows you to compare the actual cash amounts over a period of time rather than pouring over the results of a single year. If one number looks either very large or very small, you should research the details of that account. This system allows you to take a hard look at your expenditures on a year-to-year basis to get some idea of where they may be out of time.

The example I have used in Figure 8.1 shows a company with 1991 sales revenue of $1.8 million. It is easy to see that the sales have fallen by 20 percent over the three years that are covered by this report. The owner of any business who has experienced this drop in

FIGURE 8.1
FINANCIAL ANALYSIS, INCOME STATEMENT

Accounts	1991	1992	1993
Sales	$1,800,000.00	$1,600,000.00	$1,450,000.00
Cost of Goods Sold	$1,260,000.00	$1,136,000.00	$1,044,000.00
Gross Profit	$540,000.00	$464,000.00	$406,000.00
Expenses:			
Wages	$305,000.00	$285,000.00	$262,000.00
Benefits	$18,000.00	$20,500.00	$22,500.00
Rent	$23,000.00	$23,000.00	$23,000.00
Utilities	$6,500.00	$6,800.00	$7,100.00
Sales Expenses	$45,000.00	$54,000.00	$38,000.00
Telephone	$23,000.00	$19,500.00	$16,500.00
Insurance	$6,000.00	$6,200.00	$5,800.00
Depreciation	$7,500.00	$6,800.00	$5,900.00
Interest Expense	$20,000.00	$16,000.00	$12,000.00
Office Expenses	$30,000.00	$40,000.00	$35,000.00
Warehouse Expenses	$15,000.00	$21,000.00	$18,500.00
Total Expenses	$499,000.00	$498,800.00	$446,300.00
Net Profit (loss) before tax	$41,000.00	($34,800.00)	($40,300.00)
Debt Repayment (Begining of year)	**Debt**	**Debt**	**Debt**
$250,000 @ 8% for 5 years	$200,000.00		
$200,000 @ 8% for 4 years		$150,000.00	
$150,000 @ 8% for 3 years			$150,000.00

1992 sold some assets to pay debt
1993 unable to pay any principal

revenue is already aware of it, and his first instinct might be to stop here and not analyze further. He may walk around believing that if only he could increase his sales, all his problems would be over.

The line-to-line chart in this example does send up several areas to investigate. A year-to-year comparison shows growing costs of benefits that should be looked at more closely. Wages are down (note that the amount is less than the 20 percent of revenue loss) but also important is that the cost of benefits are up. These two numbers should increase or decrease at the same time. There may be other glaring inconsistencies on your own statement—take a hard look at the details.

Convert Numbers to Percentages

Step 2 is to transform these numbers into their percentage form (Figure 8.2). Each number is converted to a percentage of the total amount of expense. With your numbers in this format, you can compare both your profit margins and expenses on a year-to-year basis.

Studying a report such as this may help you find the answers to what ails your company. Are your profit margins remaining steady, or are they dropping? Are the problems in the gross profit margins or are your administrative costs too high for your current level of sales?

If at least one of the three years that you are using as a comparison wasn't a year of healthy profits, go back and find the last year that did make a net profit. Restate the figures from that period to conform with the ones on your chart and use it as a model.

Figure 8.2 of my example is a very telling document. The very first thing I notice is that the cost of goods (which should be a stable percentage) has gone up and the profit percentage has gone down. The gross profit is 2 percent less in 1993 than in 1991. This factor alone would have wiped out most of 1991 net (before taxes). The major point to consider here is that if this company's sales grow back to earlier levels they will still be in jeopardy.

This chart shows that there are a number of other very important areas to investigate and improve. Wages have become far too high as a percentage of costs. In 1991 the total percentage of wages and benefits were almost 60 percent of expenses; now they total 70 percent. Have salaries gone up while revenue has gone down? Are there too many managers on the payroll?

Also, in this example is evidence that the office and warehouse costs as a percentage of expense have gotten out of line. In 1991, they totaled 8.25 percent of expense, but by 1993, they total almost 13.25

FIGURE 8.2
FINANCIAL ANALYSIS, INCOME STATEMENT PERCENTAGES

Accounts	1991	1992	1993
Sales	100.00%	100.00%	100.00%
Cost of Goods Sold	70.00%	71.00%	72.00%
Gross Profit	30.00%	29.00%	28.00%
Expenses:			
Wages	56.48%	61.42%	64.53%
Benefits	3.33%	4.42%	5.54%
Rent	4.26%	4.96%	5.67%
Utilities	1.20%	1.47%	1.75%
Sales Expenses	8.33%	11.64%	9.36%
Telephone	4.26%	4.20%	4.06%
Insurance	1.11%	1.34%	1.43%
Depreciation	1.39%	1.47%	1.45%
Interest Expense	3.70%	3.45%	2.96%
Office Expenses	5.56%	8.62%	8.62%
Warehouse Expenses	2.78%	4.53%	4.56%
Total Expenses	92.41%	107.50%	109.93%
Net Profit (loss) before tax	7.59%	-7.50%	-9.93%

percent, an increase of about 60 percent! You may not have seen this in the raw numbers, but it becomes very obvious in the percent conversion chart.

Make a Line-by-Line Analysis

Step 3 of this process is to make a line-by-line analysis (Figure 8.3). Review areas where you are performing well, not just areas where there are problems. Note that I have made a comment on every line of my example, and you should do the same. It will force you to pay attention to all the aspects of your operation even if you did not normally do so on a regular basis. Ask others in your company to explain their own areas of responsibility. Any questions raised must be investigated further.

I have made comments along the lines described in my review for the early analysis statements, but in Figure 8.3, I have added a few more. The sales expense described here has been going down in numbers even though it is up as a percentage. I would want to consider whether this company's marketing efforts are sufficient to generate the new sales they need.

Also, I have noted under the insurance category that the company should go out and seek competitive bids. In this case, I was hoping to create some steps to be taken to bring this operation back into line. All the managers should have a copy of this chart.

See If You Are at or above Break-even

One other serious issue to consider is what your current break-even (no loss/no profit) revenue number is. This is the level of revenue you *must* have at your current profit margin to pay all your current expenses.

To find your approximate break-even number on a monthly basis, you divide your total expenses from the past year by 12. While accepted accounting principles would have you consider the payment of interest and taxes as "below the line" items not to be considered as general expense, for the purpose of a turnaround, you should add them.

Next you need to establish your average profit margin percentage on sales (gross profit minus net sales). For example, if your gross profit on $1,000,000 of sales is $300,000, then your percentage margin is 30 percent. If your total expense is $750,000, you will need $2,500,000 to break even (expense divided by gross profit percentage). See the Break-even Work Sheet in Figure 8.4.

FIGURE 8.3
FINANCIAL ANALYSIS, INCOME STATEMENT WITH COMMENTS

Accounts	1991	1992	1993	Comments
Sales	100.00%	100.00%	100.00%	
Cost of Goods Sold	70.00%	71.00%	72.00%	cost have increased
Gross Profit	30.00%	29.00%	28.00%	down by 2% (cost/profit)
Expenses:				
Wages	56.48%	61.42%	64.53%	up by over 10%
Benefits	3.33%	4.42%	5.54%	too high to sustain
Rent	4.26%	4.96%	5.67%	more sales will handle
Utilities	1.20%	1.47%	1.75%	high but not out of control
Sales Expenses	8.33%	11.64%	9.36%	are we spending enough
Telephone	4.26%	4.20%	4.06%	O.K.
Insurance	1.11%	1.34%	1.43%	get bids
Depreciation	1.39%	1.47%	1.45%	fixed amount - no cash loss
Interest Expense	3.70%	3.45%	2.96%	refinance at lower rate?
Office Expenses	5.56%	8.62%	8.62%	too high!
Warehouse Expenses	2.78%	4.53%	4.56%	needs serious analysis
Total Expenses	92.41%	107.50%	109.93%	
Net Profit (loss) before tax	7.59%	-7.50%	-9.93%	trend is dangerous

FIGURE 8.4.
BREAK-EVEN WORK SHEET

Example 1

Overhead Expense

Rent

Utilities

Wages

Office expense

Insurance

Taxes

Interest

(Any other expense *except* depreciation)

	$750,000
Gross profit margin	30%

30% of $2,500,000 = $750,000

Example 2 (from Figure 8.1)

1992 Statement

Expenses = $492,000 (less depreciation)

Gross margin 29%: 29% of $1,700,000 = $493,000

If the break-even number you have calculated is possible to reach, you may try to grow your way out of your present circumstance. If the sales number seems remote, then consider how to lower it by raising profits and lowering expense. However, it is important to focus on one thing at a time. Don't take the shotgun approach of trying to change everything all at the same time.

THE FOUR MOST LIKELY PROBLEM AREAS TO REVIEW

1. Overall sales volume
2. Gross profit margin (pricing)

3. Overhead expense
4. Debt service (interest expense and principal payment)

Has Your Overall Sales Volume Decreased?

Whether your industry is downsizing or experiencing a period of flat growth, changing times as well as changing buying patterns will put pressure on your overall gross revenue. With less money coming in, there is inevitably less to be allocated to pay bills, and that creates pain. Your sales will not come back on their own—opportunities for new sales will increase during a general economic recovery, but your company will still have to pursue new sources of revenue.

Take a realistic look at where your markets have been in the past and who your customers are as well as how their buying habits may have changed to determine where new sales may be found. Then analyze your current position. Is the overall market you serve growing or fairly static? Can you increase your revenue by adding new product lines? Is the only way you can increase your volume to severely cut prices? Can you exist on low margin sales? What marketing costs will be involved in producing new sales?

As I've said earlier, assuming that higher sales are the answer to everything that will result in an instant turnaround is a mistake. If you are at break-even and your gross profits are stable, additional revenue at current or even lower margins will surely help. But if your profit margins are too low, increased volume may result in higher losses and bring you closer to your demise. Consider this as only one piece of the puzzle.

If the company profiled in Figure 8.2 sells more at current operating costs, their losses will only increase. The airline industry constantly fills seats at less than cost believing that their overall revenue gain will ultimately help. What has been happening in reality is that full-price customers have been using lower-cost tickets and the red ink continues to flow. If you are giving your product away (not making any profit)—stop now and overhaul your entire operation.

Are Your Gross Profit Margins Sufficient?

If your gross profit margins seem very low or are on a steady decline on a year-to-year comparison, that may be the real culprit in your case. You should measure your company against industry averages (these numbers are available through trade associations and in published works, the major one by Robert Morris Associates) and determine how close your actual profit margins are to similar size companies in your field or industry.

If you have been very aggressive in the market to spur on early fast growth, you may now find your business grossly underpricing its goods or services. However, if you have been a supplier to others long enough to establish a satisfied and somewhat loyal customer base, now may be the time to phase in a price increase. A small manufacturer I worked with in my own business always took work at low margins because he wanted to achieve rapid growth. Not only was he often the low bidder, but his service was exceptional because he (and his crew) were willing to work long hours and over weekends to meet customers' demand. After keeping the same price list for three years, he reluctantly raised everything by at least 5 percent and worried about what would happen to his volume. At that point, due in great part to his fine reputation, it continued to increase.

Pricing of a product or service is part science and part art. You should not be afraid of charging a fair price, but you should be aware of where your competition is and how it will affect your overall revenue. Some price increases result in lower volume. However, lower volume at higher margins can in fact be more desirable. Thirty percent gross of $1 million is $300,000, and 20 percent gross of $1.2 million is $240,000. Which profit figure would you prefer?

Is Your Overhead in Line with Revenues?

It is easy to become accustomed to the monthly bills you incur and not think too much about whether or not they are in line with your revenue or how you would be able to reduce them. At some point, your revenue must cover all your fixed expenses (rent, utilities, administrative wages, interest, etc.) and that may not have represented a problem to you in previous years. However, if your sales fall or your profit margins drop, just meeting these obligations can become an ongoing nightmare. This is one of the issues you must analyze. If your overhead percentage is growing and taking with it all your profits, this is an area for further analysis and corrective action, which will be covered in detail in Chapter 9.

Is Your Current Debt Service Too High?

Perhaps you are still paying off your start-up loans, and your growth hasn't been as fast as you had predicted at the outset. Few businesses meet their own rosy projections. You may have incurred debt for an expansion that didn't show the accompanying increase in sales that you had projected. Most difficult of all, you may have been borrowing operating capital and now be at the end of your credit line and unable to pay it back out of current cash flow. Be tough on yourself when you consider your debt situation. Too high a debt load is serious but not impossible to solve. What it will require will be tough negotiations and perhaps legal advice. Chapter 10 discusses this issue in detail.

You need to determine, as well, whether your goal is to reduce debt to meet your current operating levels or to plan to grow enough so that revenues will increase to meet debt. I have worked with companies that have made each one of these choices, and they both are possible. What is required from you is a realistic assessment of your company and its potential. Is the demand for your product or service growing? Are you competitive enough to get a bigger share of your market? Ask tough questions; the answers are important.

DETERMINE WHAT NEEDS TO BE CHANGED TO BECOME PROFITABLE AGAIN

If you have effectively analyzed your comparative statements, you should have a handle on where the problems are centered and where you should put your priorities. Over the next several chapters, we will look at how to focus on some of the most likely areas of problems and how to begin to develop a plan of action for change.

SUMMING UP

Take the time to review company operations before planning your next step. Follow these guidelines:

1. Spread three years of statements side by side.
2. Do a percentage analysis as well.
3. Compare on a line-by-line basis.
4. Determine if gross profits are high enough.
5. Analyze overhead.
6. Review all current debt.
7. Determine your break-even revenue.

CHAPTER

9

Review Your Overhead Expenses

If you have analyzed your statements and believe that your gross profits are in line but your expenses (fixed or variable) are too high, that's where your attention should be focused next. In the first stage of your turnaround, you may have responded to the need to cut all expenses for a short period of time. But now for the long haul, what you should do is change the focus and identify the costs that are out of line and determine how to reduce them and keep them down permanently.

MAKE A DETAILED REVIEW OF EACH LINE ITEM

Take a hard look at what individual items are included in every line item even if you think you already know what they are. Look at them even if you believe that they can't be altered. You may have assumed that expenses such as rent are just a fact of life, but that isn't always the case. You should take a look at what you are paying per square foot, and then review how much of your space is really needed. You may have moved into space with an idea to expand, and now you need to contract. Now is the time to face this reality, and in Part III, we will begin to develop strategies to lower costs in every category.

Even Fixed Costs Can Be Cut

As you complete your overhead review, other line item expenses such as rent that you view as fixed costs should be considered. It may be possible to reduce the cost of your telephone service or other utility. Administrative wages may appear to be an absolute necessity before you begin this process, but there are savings in this area also. Even if you can't at the moment think of any way to create a savings, if you see any cost that you believe to be high, make a note of it and give some attention to a plan to save money in that area.

One of my clients had very high employment costs (e.g., unemployment tax, worker's compensation, and insurance). He was aware that these costs were preventing his business from being competitive on quotes, and the lost business was seriously affecting his bottom line. After much investigation, we found an employment leasing company whose business was to hire my client's employees, pay their wages and benefits, and lease them back for a fee. The leasing company enjoyed a substantial benefit in costs (on unemployment tax as well as a good insurance package) and the whole process *saved* 10 percent—enough to make a difference. This type of service is operating in most major cities.

How to Determine the Value of Your Sales Expense

Sales and marketing expense may seem to be very flexible costs, and it can be difficult to determine the exact value of many of these activities. This category will include items such as

- Advertising
- Promotions
- Travel
- Entertainment
- Printing and mailing marketing material

At a time when cash is short, it may be all too easy to make serious cuts in these areas, and it could end up as a serious mistake.

Current clients need to see and hear from you, and the only way to develop prospective customers is to get the opportunity to let them know about your company and its product or service.

Any analysis of your current costs in these areas must be done with an understanding of what your competition does along the lines of advertising or entertainment so that you can stay prominent in your customers' eyes.

As I look back on my 21 years in industrial manufacturing, I now realize that I did far too little entertaining. It happened because early on it wasn't easy for a woman to take one man or a group of men out for dinner or a sporting event. Over the years, it became easier, but I never developed the habit. When business was soft, my competition that had a greater presence got more of the orders than my company did. It's an important effort to make.

COST PER CUSTOMER OR PER TRANSACTION You can measure your sales expense on a cost per customer or cost per transaction basis. The choice you make should depend on the type of business you operate and the market you serve. If you sell to a limited number of customers, use cost per customer. Otherwise, use the cost-per-transaction basis. The formula would be the following:

Average monthly sales expense divided by average number of sales.

For example, if your average expense is $2,500 and you have 500 sales, then your cost per transaction is $5.00. Compare that to the average value of each sale. If your monthly gross volume is $75,000, divide that by 500, and you will find that your average sale is $150. Your $5.00 transaction cost translates into a sales cost of 3 percent. If your profit margin is 25 percent, this may be reasonable; if your margins are 10 percent (such as a travel agency), this may be high and will have to be addressed. Conversely, if the number is very low, perhaps you aren't doing enough to promote your company. You know what your customers demand and what expenditure may be necessary to develop new accounts so this is a call for your own instincts. Balance good marketing with cash conservation.

REVIEW YOUR ADMINISTRATIVE COSTS

You must also measure your administrative costs against a fixed productivity factor just as you measure your sales expense. How much overhead cost are you maintaining to transact your day-to-day business? You might translate it to a cost per order that should include processing the order, billing it, recording all aspects of the transaction, and ultimately collecting the account and making your own payments to cover the costs of your operation. Your own salary (or at least a portion of it) as well as other managers' wages are also part of this cost. Divide your total overhead by the number of transactions to find out a cost per order. Then you must decide if this expense to handle the administrative business is in line or too high. Streamlining your operating procedures or outsourcing some of this work is a way to cut the cost; others will be considered in Part III of this book.

Involve Your Managers in Overhead Review

If your company has a talented controller or office or general manager, he or she can be the point person in a cost–benefit analysis. You first want to determine which items should be put up for scrutiny and then delegate the research. Once you begin considering what course of action must be taken, you should make the decision process inclusive with the individuals whose department will be involved. The leadership is yours, but the contributions from others should be solicited and considered.

Remember that the managers involved in reviewing overhead costs may be impacted by the decisions you make, so they may be inclined to pull punches and not give you their most candid opinions. No one likes to have their budgets reduced or, worse yet, their jobs eliminated. If you are aware of an overhead area that may require very serious and deep cuts, you should be up front with the managers whose job security may be in jeopardy. Perhaps they can move to a different assignment, or you may still be able to ask them to help if you allow those who will be impacted to seek other employment opportunities while the changes are ongoing. It will be easier for them to find a new job while they are still employed. Your sensitivity and respect for others during tough times will be long remembered. On the other hand, your secrecy or lack of loyalty will also be remembered by those who stay.

Don't Create Unnecessarily High Stress

It is never easy to face difficulty and find solutions. The early stages of awareness are confusing, and everyone is concerned about the outcome. For your employees, the stress is also felt deeply and can become serious and cause conflict between people who should be working together to achieve a single positive outcome.

If you engage in finger pointing—that is, accusing others in your organization of spending too much money—you won't be creating the atmosphere conducive to finding solutions. Your job is to determine where the problems are and correct them. It's in everyone's self-interest to work for the future, not recriminate about the past.

Some Costs Are Subject to Legal Constraints

Your business will have fixed monthly expenses that are covered by legal agreements and binding contracts such as rental agreements, equipment leases and supply contracts, and labor agreements. And the costs covered by one or more of these may be just the expense that is burdening your company.

However, in some instances, not only are the contracts legally binding, but they may have cancellation penalties or payment acceleration clauses that make them very expensive to rescind. Now is the time to seek the advice of an attorney. First, you will want to understand the actual costs of these clauses (few of us review them in advance), and second, you will want to know if there is a way to avoid this type of penalty. Contracts often contain escape clauses for various types of nonperformance and to activate them may require documentation on your part over a period of time. Check it out now so you will be ready when the time comes to take action.

INCREASE PRODUCTIVITY AND YOU WILL INCREASE PROFIT

While you are considering how to cut costs, you should also be looking at ways to increase productivity. If output goes up, cost per item or transaction goes down. Don't neglect this consideration as you make your review.

Can your salespeople increase the number of calls they make? Can they help out with administrative or shipping duties? Can general office staff increase their tasks to include work normally done by part-time staff or outside service? If you manufacture, can your factory use idle time to produce products as subcontract work for others?

Is there work for others that you can take in to increase your output per employee?

These are a few of the questions you should be asking yourself. When looking at overhead, don't just use a slash and burn approach to reducing costs. Use a surgical knife, not a machete, and if you combine this approach with an increase in sales and/or margins, you can achieve some dramatic results.

REVIEW ALL YOUR DEBT

From start-up loans to equipment or auto loans to short-term lines of credit, it is not unusual for a company to have several loans that it is paying on at one time. You may be paying interest only on a demand note or a fixed principal and interest payment on term loans, but they all should be reviewed.

Although the basic rule is that a company should not borrow money unless it has the profits to pay back the principal, many start-up loans are granted with the expectation of future earnings. At times, your bank may be willing to make a short-term line of credit available to smooth over the rough spots. Many companies find themselves unable to retire these notes, and they turn them into a term loan with a regularly scheduled payment. If the profits don't return, these loans can become a real burden to your cash flow. Something has to be done. The debt may jeopardize the entire business.

The most difficult case I've seen was a contractor who started with an equipment loan of $150,000, went on to a $300,000 line of credit for working capital, and ended up with over $500,000 of debt. Payments squeezed his cash flow enough that he wasn't able to pay many of his subcontractors, and they made claims on his bonds. We began to work on the debt load very late and weren't able to restructure any of his loans so that the company could generate the needed cash flow to continue operations. I believe that even six months earlier, there were options to pursue that eroded with time. He was forced to sell out to a major construction firm to avoid bankruptcy.

Four Questions to Consider in Reviewing Your Debt

There are four main question to ask and answer in analyzing loans:

1. What is the current debt total?
2. What interest rate are you paying?

3. How many payments remain?
4. Is it secured?

Create a chart like the one shown in Figure 9.1 to list all these elements of your debt.

FIGURE 9.1

Loan No. (type)	Amount Due ($)	Interest Rate (%)	Payments Remain (no.)	Secured Yes

WHAT IS THE TOTAL AMOUNT OF YOUR DEBT? Your review of total debt is important to determine the solvency of your company. If you have a mortgage that belongs to the company or lease purchases for equipment that can't be canceled, include them in your total debt. An analysis is only valuable if it is complete.

WHAT INTEREST RATE ARE YOU PAYING? Do you know the interest rate on each loan, including any lease–purchase deal you may have? If your company is still paying on older loan instruments that were not pegged to prime, these may have rates far higher than are currently available. Virtually all leases are at a high rate because they aren't issued by the primary source of the funds. Lease companies borrow money themselves and must add a few percentage points as their own profit margin. Consider the effects of a lower interest rate on your monthly payment.

WHEN DOES THE LOAN MATURE? You will also want to consider the term (length of time) that your loan was originally written to cover. The shorter the term, the higher the monthly payment. Stretching out a loan for a longer time may curb your ability to borrow additional funds for the near term, but you could substantially increase your cash flow by increasing the term and making lower monthly payments. You could use the extra cash for increased marketing efforts that would have long-term benefits.

ARE THE LOANS SECURED? As you review your loans, you should also determine whether they are secured or not. If the lender has a lien on a specific piece of equipment, then determine whether the value of the equipment currently is less than, more than, or equal to the current balance of the loan. A loan that was written to cover all general assets may have been considered secured at the time but may not be now if the value of those assets is less than the current balance of the loan.

For example, if a loan was written at a time you had $150,000 of receivables and $100,000 of inventory, it was secured at that time. If after a period of poor business conditions, your receivables are now only $80,000 and your inventory only $50,000, then any loan portion over $130,000 is actually unsecured. This is important to know because any court-ordered reorganization will likely force your lender to accept less for any portion of its loan that is no longer secured and it knows that. You may need this information as a negotiating tool.

By this point, you have done a thorough examination of the current operation of your business. Now it may seem to be the time to roll up your sleeves and dive in to make all sorts of decisions and changes. But wait—don't do anything yet.

KNOW WHERE YOU'RE GOING BEFORE YOU BEGIN

It's impossible not to be impressed by the military success of Desert Storm, and it should be a guiding lesson about strategic planning. The troops were in the country for months before the offensive began, and the win was a stunning one. Even if you think you know exactly what needs to be done—you may have really known for some time but just didn't do anything about it, don't start before your whole plan is developed.

Decide what your goals are and determine your priorities—that is, what has to happen before your company is once again nurtured back to health. Your analysis should have highlighted the major areas for concern—the chapters ahead will give you ideas on how to correct each of the problems you need to address.

SUMMING UP

When you begin to analyze your current overhead costs you should consider the following steps:

1. Get a detailed review on each line item to see where you can save expense.
2. Review all fixed costs even those such as rent that you believe can't be changed.
3. Determine cost of marketing and sales expense that you spend per customer.
4. Analyze your administrative cost per sale.
5. Include managers in both the analysis and implementation of any plan.
6. Keep the stress level in check; everyone in the organization may be feeling under siege.
7. Consider all your debt—the total amount as well as the interest rates and the terms.
8. Develop a plan for corrections before taking any action or making radical changes.

CHAPTER

10

Review Your Marketing Plan

If you have determined that, for the most part, your costs are in line or that your current overhead will be almost impossible to reduce substantially, the company may have to grow its way out of the current crisis. If your profit margin is adequate, what you will need to do is to revisit and possibly redefine your current market strategy and then increase your marketing efforts.

Your company should have a written marketing plan, and if you don't have one, that's the place to start. Develop the plan in cooperation with the members of your staff that have marketing and sales responsibility.

THE BASIC ELEMENTS OF YOUR MARKETING PLAN

There are a number of areas you need to review before revising your current strategy or creating a new one.

1. Who are your best customers?

2. What are the features and benefits of your company that make customers choose you over the competition?
3. Are there other customers of the same type that you could attract?
4. What is the best way to make them aware of your business?
5. How can you develop a cost-effective strategy to accomplish the task?

Who Are Your Best Customers?

Many businesses open their doors to manufacture or sell a product or service without knowing exactly who their target customers will be. If that scenario has been a part of your company's history, you know how difficult it can be to try and market yourself to virtually everyone without having a specific customer type in mind. And even if you did know exactly who your customers were when you started your company, after a company has been in business for any length of time, the customer base may have changed dramatically.

The manufacturing company I operated for 21 years produced and sold safety products to industrial end users. Since I took over a business with existing clients, I didn't think that I would have to devote much time to the consideration of where our customer base really was. Within ten years after I took over the operation, almost 50 percent of our original customers had closed completely or experienced serious cutbacks. By the time I realized that I had to find almost an entire new set of customers, it was almost too late.

I have worked with a small retailer who had been selling the same type of merchandise for years while the neighborhood where he was located changed dramatically. All the demographics including race and age were now different. He was friendly and well liked, but no one wanted the type of goods he carried. A complete revamping was required to bring his business back to life.

When is the last time you reviewed where your sales were originating and determined what information you could derive from your current sales data? Unlike a start-up, you now have a business history to use as a basis for some in-depth analysis of your customer base. What common traits can you identify among those who have chosen to do business with your company? Use the demographic checklist in Figure 10.1 to draw your customer profile.

FIGURE 10-1
A DEMOGRAPHIC CHECKLIST

If you sell to other businesses,

- What is your customer size—large companies or small businesses?
- Where are they located—regional or national?
- What type of business are they in?
- What is their management structure—do they have a purchasing department?

If you sell to individuals,

- What are the ages of your customers?
- What are their marital status and family size?
- What is their family income level?
- What is their education level?
- What is their ethnicity?
- What is their geographical drawing area?

By drawing a profile of those who have made the buying decision in favor of your company, you will find a road map to finding the most likely new clients.

What Benefits Make Customers Choose Your Company?

If you're the chief salesperson for your business, then you should understand what is special and unique about your company. As you may know, these may *not* be the main drawing feature that cause others to patronize you. You may believe that your restaurant has the best food in town, but your customers may come because you are close. Once you have your customer profile, then you should be able to analyze why they have chosen you. Is it a special product line? Service or training that you give along with your product? Fast delivery? Convenient location? Are you the lowest price in town?

There are two or three main reasons that you have attracted your existing clientele and you want to determine what they are so that you can expand your marketing efforts and begin to grow again. Even if the answers aren't readily apparent to you, all you have to do is ask.

You do it in the form of a market survey that can be done by you or you can hire a marketing firm to conduct your survey, although this can be expensive. Four students from a business school spent a semester on this type of project for me, and their insights were excellent. The value of students is that most people will readily speak to them and tend to give candid answers. I even found out why some people didn't do business with my company. You can register to become a project of a business class or go out on your own and hire business students to work on your survey. These are answers you need because they form the base of your strategy.

Are There Additional Customers to Develop?

The next phase of your analysis is to determine whether you can continue to grow by developing new customers similar to the ones you have or whether you will have to change your business in some meaningful way. For example, if you already have a major portion of your existing market (e.g., 40 percent of all the pizzas in your area are bought from your shop), then you are going to have to be innovative to increase your sales. It could be something as basic as enlarging your existing product line or services you offer, or you may have to expand your location or open a new one.

If, on the other hand, you have only a tiny portion of the available business, while this fact may be personally frustrating to you, the good side is that there is a lot of room to grow. Aggressive sales and marketing campaigns should work for you. Expanding your revenue will in many cases turn your business back to profit. Before you begin, you must be convinced that an expansion is possible without massive infusions of capital. If it will take an expensive advertising or promotion budget and you don't have the money, then it might be impossible to attract the new customers you need.

What Is the Best Way to Attract the Attention of New Customers?

Does your company have in place a program of regular communications with your existing customers? If your answer to that question is no, I can almost guarantee that your company does not have a plan to develop new customers. If you have reviewed the potential opportunities for expansion and determined that growth is critical for your survival and future, a plan should be a high priority with you at this time.

There is much written material about various types of marketing, the "guerrilla" or low-cost type as well as the top of the line. Since your company may not be in a position at this time to throw money at a problem, you will want to choose both your method and its implementation with great care. Regardless of the direction you choose, the first step is to decide to whom (what type of potential customer) you are talking and what message (the important features of your company) they should be hearing. Again, this is work that can be done by others, but if cost is the issue, it can be done by you and your existing staff. You are developing a targeted market to go after.

There are a wide variety of methods to raise awareness of your company to the customers you are looking to attract. The following list should give you some ideas of the alternatives you could consider.

- Advertising—General
  Direct mail
  Brochures
  Yellow Pages
  Newspaper
  Radio and TV
  Signs on your building and vehicles
- One-to-One Promotion
  Personal letters
  Special discounts
  Telemarketing
  Canvassers
  Direct sales calls
- Public Relations
  Joining organizations
  Tip clubs
  Speaking opportunities
  Supporting a team or an event

These should trigger some ideas for you, and you should pursue the ones that seem to be most appropriate for *both* your message *and* the customer you are trying to reach.

Is There a Cost-effective Way to Market Your Company?

Finally, you should decide what cost per sale or cost per new customer would be acceptable so that you can set a budget for your marketing efforts. Determine the profitability of each new customer or additional sale and determine what amount of that profit potential should be committed to new customer development.

If you have earned profits of $50,000 on the cumulative sales to 500 active accounts, your average profit per existing customer is $100. It would be imprudent to spend $10,000 to develop 50 new accounts at this time because these new accounts would end up costing you $200 each, and it would take years to earn back your investment. Your goals now are a faster return on your dollar expenditure. In the future, long-range development projects are always worth consideration. For now, keep the expense to less than 20 percent of your expected return. You need to earn profit, not spend it.

Don't be deterred by a low budget. With desktop publishing capabilities and cable television channels, all sorts of marketing concepts are possible at a fraction of what they once would have cost. Instead of giving up or giving in to spending money you don't have, take the time to read one of the many books available on low-cost marketing or take a course at your community college. Once you get into the middle of a spirited campaign, you will probably find it to be more fun than you assume. You're in business because you believe in what you do. Here's your chance to tell others about that belief.

PROJECT A POSITIVE IMAGE

While you are analyzing your current market position, deciding if your major efforts should go in that direction, and developing a strategy, keep in mind that to neglect any marketing is a serious mistake. If your decision is to focus on the internal workings of your company, don't concentrate on that issue to the complete neglect of the image and message you are transmitting to existing as well as potential customers.

When a company gets into some difficulty, that fact often becomes common knowledge. If you do not develop a plan for at least some external communication, customers will begin to wonder what your long-term intentions are. This can be prevented by a program of regular communication and promotion of new products and new ideas.

SUMMING UP

Take an analytical view of how your company is marketing to new and existing customers.

1. Do you know who your best customers are?
2. Are you promoting the most important feature of your business?
3. As your company currently operates now, are there new market opportunities?
4. Can you design a cost-effective marketing program?
5. Customer communication is an important component of a successful business.

CHAPTER

11

When to Bring an Outside Consultant on Board

Many entrepreneurs are specialists in one aspect of their business, and if the thought of doing all this analysis and making tough decisions as a result is more of a task than you feel like attempting alone at this time, you may want to find a consultant to assist in this project. If you believe that the objectivity of an outsider would be of value, this is a move worth careful consideration. The following are a number of the specific tasks you may require assistance to accomplish.

- Determining the problem areas.
- Setting new priorities.
- Developing a strategy.
- Implementing the plan.

DETERMINING WHERE THE PROBLEMS EXIST

Entrepreneurs frequently become so involved in the day-to-day operation of their own business that drawing back to get an objective view becomes difficult. You may have devoted time in one area of your operation and put together a talented team of managers and employees to complete other tasks. However, because of changes in the business environment around you, an area unfamiliar to you may be where serious changes must be made. You may be very astute to understand your own quandary over completing an objective analysis of how costs can be cut or improvements can be made.

Very few entrepreneurs are specialists in all areas of business from marketing to production to finances. Often, there is one area of interest and skill that is the driving force for starting a business, and if a strong team isn't formed to handle the other aspects of operations, many of the problems develop in those areas. It is quite difficult for the owner who has little interest in finance to review his own performance in that area or a contractor who loves to work outside and build to make a serious analysis of his company's marketing strategy. In fact, the company may not even have one. This is clearly a case where outside advice can be of great value.

SETTING PRIORITIES AND DEVELOPING A STRATEGY

Once you know what areas require attention, you will have to establish your priorities and determine how you will implement any needed changes. Some of the work required may be time- and energy-consuming, and this may be difficult for you to accomplish at the same time you are completing your day-to-day work.

The instinct of the business owner is to plan for an immediate turnaround. You may have been dealing with your difficulties for many months or even years, and now you want it to be over quickly. Setting reasonable priorities and time lines as well as the strategy to accomplish your plan may be very much beyond the stress and impatience that you are currently feeling. The assistance of an outsider in this phase may help.

IMPLEMENTING THE PLAN

The last phase of your turnaround will be the implementation of your plan for change. This phase may involve selling off assets, calling creditors, closing unprofitable operations, laying off employees, increasing prices, collecting past due accounts from customers, or changing vendors. Some of these tasks can be very cumbersome from a personal perspective, and attempting them alone, you may wish to put them off longer than you should.

Any time change is brought to an organization, there are feelings of guilt, frustration, and sometimes outright anger that are experienced by everyone, including the owner. Finger pointing can happen, with employees believing that the owner made all the mistakes and the owner feeling that no one in his employ cares as much as he does. The truth, of course, is that most likely both have done some things quite well and both have made some mistakes. Everyone can feel the stress and an outsider may be able to take the brunt of it and keep those who are working together from confronting each other. This can be particularly true when a business involves a married couple or a family. The value of outside help is in moving forward into the implementation rather than trying to relive what went wrong.

These are very good reasons to hire an outside consultant to work with you. Once you have made the decision, where do you find the best consultant for your operation and how much will it cost? These two issues are connected because there are places to find very low- or actually no-cost advisors and there are consultants who charge a fairly high rate usually comparable to a lawyer's fee. Your goal is to balance the two and find someone who is cost effective.

There are a variety of places to look for help and these three are good sources to consider:

1. Local colleges or universities
2. Local and federal agencies
3. Listings of private consultants

Finding Help at Universities

You may be able to find undergraduate business students or even MBA candidates to do work for you at no cost. I have worked with both and found value in their projects. Needless to say, the MBA students are more astute and can tackle more complex problems. The down side of using students is that they need a certain amount of supervision, but the good news is that the energy and enthusiasm of a student can be infectious.

If you can find an individual student who wishes to use your company for case study for perhaps part of his or her MBA requirements, you may really hit the jackpot. The project may last three to five months, and it is the equivalent of having a valuable unpaid employee. The most critical aspect for you will be to agree on exactly what work should be accomplished and for you to give your intern the time and attention as well as complete data to make the job worthwhile.

Also available at selected universities are Small Business Development Centers funded by the Small Business Administration. Operated by faculty members as well as hired professionals, each has a variety of programs to offer. The centers give a variety of courses as well as one-on-one counseling. The service given here will be free or low-cost, but the work is meant to be short-term. If what you are looking for is some feedback on decisions you are considering, this may be the right place. For longer projects, you will have to look elsewhere.

Getting Help from Public Agencies

The SBA operates a counseling program called SCORE (Service Corps of Retired Executives), which offers free help to any business owner who requests it. The volunteers have retired from their own business careers and are willing to work with small business owners as long as they are needed. A word of caution here is that not all the volunteers are equally qualified, and those with less ability are not refused participation in the program. If you are assigned a counselor who you feel doesn't have anything of substance to contribute, you will have to terminate the relationship. If the thought of having to "fire" a volunteer makes you uncomfortable, this may not be the program for you.

Another place to find free assistance is the development authority in your city or, in some instances, your local neighborhoods. Many of these quasi-government agencies have business development specialists who can help with technical assistance or referrals and may even be able to assist you with loan programs that you could not access on your own.

Start with your city agency and ask if they have technical assistance programs for small business owners. They may refer you to a development group in your community. If you are interested in moving your business (perhaps to save some money), call the agency in the community you are considering. You will be pleasantly surprised to learn how enthusiastic they are to attract new jobs to their neighborhood. Few of these agencies have actual loan funds available, but they can help you put together a package to find loans from a variety of sources.

If you are a woman business owner or the member of a minority group, there may be a special agency or association whose main purpose is to work with nontraditional entrepreneurs. Check your local phone book or call the minority enterprise office of your state.

Using Private Consultants

Here is where the costs jump dramatically as private consultants charge by the hour and fees can run anywhere from $75 to $175 per hour. There is no shortage of business consultants available at this time since many former corporate managers who have found themselves separated from their previous jobs have decided to start consulting practices. The range of their backgrounds can be very different and not all are equal. A good advisor can be worth far more than what he or she may charge, but the burden is on you to take the time to choose carefully. And it will also be your job to set the task, make sure time isn't wasted, and pay attention to billable hours as they mount.

HOW TO CHOOSE A GOOD CONSULTANT

This is an important decision for you to make, and you should take the time to do it carefully. Don't hire the first person who walks into your office calling themselves a consultant even if they make a good impression. Talk to at least three potential candidates and solicit general business ideas as well as specific information about the candidate and their background. You should feel free to discuss the problems of your company on a general basis and get a sense of what type of problem solving your candidate offers.

Conducting an Interview with a Consultant

The first thing to note in any interview with any professional is how the two of you hit it off. You will be working very closely together in what can be at times a relatively stressful situation so having a cordial relationship is as important as mutual respect.

You will also find that most consultants present themselves with a variety of written material although few will have anything that resembles a typical resume. You still want to know about the *individual* you will be working with and not just about the firm they come from. There are national companies that will send two, three, or four different consultants to do a single project, and I am frankly skeptical about that procedure. First, because I believe it is more costly, each one will have to come up to speed about your operation before they can be of real help. And because each individual will have his or her own level of expertise, the work may be inconsistent.

You have the right to meet with the consultant assigned to your case face to face in advance of agreeing to hire any firm. If a national or even local consulting practice is not willing to agree to this practice, I would suggest that you pass on the offer. A sole practitioner will allow you to accomplish this, but he or she may not have expertise in all the areas you require. A small, local practice may be an effective alternative. Figure 11.1 is a checklist to use when interviewing a consultant.

FIGURE 11.1
CONSULTANT INTERVIEW CHECKLIST

1. What is their personal business background?
   - Small business or corporate
   - Specialized or general business
   - Middle manager or the "one in charge"
   - Any entrepreneurial experience
2. How much consulting experience?
   - What types of projects
   - What specific results achieved
   - What types of businesses
3. What is their general business philosophy?
   - View of current business environment
   - View of business goals/personal goals
4. What references can they give about themselves, not just their firm?

Check References Carefully

You should call every name given to you as a reference by any consultant and ask them a series of detailed questions. You should not expect other business owners to give you confidential information about their companies and the work they had done, but you should expect to hear general comments. If more than one of the names on your list seems hesitant to talk, this should be a warning sign. Some of the questions to ask include the following:

1. Was the work satisfactory?

2. Did the consultant relate well to managers and employees?
3. Was the project (or series of tasks) completed on time?
4. Was the original estimate accurate?
5. Were there many add-ons (items not covered by the original scope of the work but necessary)?

This last item is critical because it may indicate that the consultant consciously bids a job with a low estimate of the project and then runs up the tab (and the time required). This does happen, but it should not be a pattern.

One way to investigate further is to ask a reference if they know of any other clients who have worked with your consultant/candidate. You can expect to get only the most satisfied client names from your candidate, but you may be able to uncover other information by doing additional research.

HOW TO WORK SUCCESSFULLY WITH A CONSULTANT

Any time you hire a professional, you should negotiate to agreement the terms of your work together. This is true for lawyers and accountants and particularly true for consultants. You would never hire an employee to do an unspecified job during an uncontrolled period of time for a fee still undetermined. You must have a clear understanding with your consultant as to the following:

1. The scope of the work
2. The length of the assignment
3. The approximate cost

Narrow the Scope to Manageable Goals

If you hire a consultant to do a complete turnaround of your company, you are talking about some very substantial expense. For a business in the $2–5 million range, this type of work could cost $30,000 to $100,000. You could expect to have someone with you on a full-time basis for a month or so and then fairly regularly after that. It is not my contention that this is not a valuable way to handle your problem because it is. There are a number of talented turnaround experts who can be of substantial value to your company. But my experience has been that few companies experiencing difficulties can afford this level of assistance.

If keeping the cost down is critical to you, then good control of your consultant starts with the scope of the job. If you are feeling that you have no clue, why not begin with an analysis of your operation that will become a report with specific recommendations. This type of assignment is short-term, and you should be quoted an absolute time and cost of this work. Depending on the complexity of your business, the work should take two to five days and cost $2,000 to $4,000. Most consultants who work with small businesses would be willing to complete this type of analysis.

Beyond this phase, the work should be specifically identified by the area to be covered and the goal of the task. Open-ended assignments can go on forever without any meaningful conclusion or result to determine their success. You don't want to become dependent on your consultant—setting goals even if they are interim goals will allow you to analyze how the work is progressing.

Set Time Frames for Completion

When someone is doing a job that is unfamiliar to you, it is hard to assess how long it will take to complete the work. That doesn't mean that you should allow a consultant to finish at their own pace.

If your car was at a mechanic's, you would want to know when it would be done, and you would ask that question when you dropped off the vehicle at the garage. Before you allow a consultant to tinker with your business, ask him or her to set a specific time for completion as well as a date for a report to be submitted.

If it is a long-term project, you should have dates for completion of phases along the way.

Time Is Money: Set a Price

Once you have determined the scope of the work and a specific time to accomplish the task, your consultant will have made an estimate of the required hours. Virtually all professionals charge by the hour, so the cost of the project will now have at least a close estimate. You may want to allow a range such as 25 to 30 hours so that additional tasks can be added if needed. However, *before* you begin, you should have a firm idea of the total cost of your project.

Put Your Agreement in Writing

Some consultants use a contract to establish the terms of their work. The only problem I have with this is that you will have to add the cost of a legal review before you sign. Make sure that you have a cancellation clause included based on items within your control such as performance, and also that there is no fee escalation clause in case of termination.

What I prefer is a letter of understanding or a proposal covering the items I have discussed: scope, time, and cost. This should also specify a cancellation policy.

SUMMING UP

The responsibility for the turnaround of your company is yours, but it can be very beneficial to find outside assistance. The items to consider when hiring a consultant are the following:

1. Determine the project that requires help.
2. Consider free help as well as paid professionals.
3. Be careful about making a choice—interview more than one candidate.
4. Learn about the individual doing the work, not just the firm they represent.
5. Check references.
6. Negotiate the scope, time, and cost of the project.

CHAPTER

12

How Your Business Reflects Your Attitude

I have been consulting with small business for over a decade, but the last few years my practice has been primarily with turnarounds, and I have adopted a very holistic view of business, particularly small business. A company is not an inanimate object, it is a community of people. Your business is a living entity, and it will most likely reflect much of your personality and attitudes. If you are an aggressive person, your company will most likely be an aggressive player in the market. Similarly, if your style is low-key, that will be evident in the way your company transacts business in a less frenetic way.

When a business faces problems, even when the situation gets to crisis proportions, the way it affects the owner will often determine what ultimately happens to the company. If you believe the problems are insurmountable, they probably will be allowed to deteriorate to that point. If you are convinced that you can overcome the challenges, you will find a way to do so. So it stands to reason that along with other analysis, you should take a look at your own attitude as well. Consider the following questions:

- Have you made accommodations for your own stress?
- Are you providing leadership for your other employees?

- Have you determined your personal goals?
- Are you still committed to your business?

EVALUATE YOUR CURRENT LEVEL OF STRESS

If this is the first time in your business career that you have faced serious business problems, the reality of the down side of business may have come as a big shock to you. Your initial reaction may very likely contain elements of anger and fear that may temporarily immobilize you. This is a critical time for your company as well. At a time when your business needs to be stabilized, you may be feeling personally out of control. If you realize that your emotional response is fairly typical, it is hoped that you can move forward to acknowledge your own stress level and find ways to ease the feelings.

Don't Blame Yourself or Others

A strong component of the stress you feel is brought on by your personal sense of guilt for not being smart enough or fast enough to prevent your business from experiencing these severe problems. For the most part, they develop over a number of years for a variety of reasons, and it is not valid to blame them all on yourself. If you allow yourself to absorb all that burden, there will be little energy left to move forward.

Finger pointing at this time is not worthwhile because it won't solve any of your problems, and it won't make it any easier to find a working strategy to turn the situation around. You need to focus your time and energy on the future, and not relive the past and take aim at yourself or others in your organization for not preventing what has happened. Even if your situation has been caused by the action of others, now is not the time to become obsessed with that fact. You have to create the scenario to move forward, not seek retribution for any wrongdoing.

On this situation, I have some hands-on experience. In the mid-1980s my business suffered almost catastrophic damage due to the actions of a competitor. I was driven to find equity and restitution in the courts. At the time, an associate gave me some good advice: "You can do business or you can do law, but you can't do both." He was right, and if I had it to do over again, I would have spent more time on the issues facing my company to overcome our problems whether they were of our creation or not.

In my consulting practice, I often come across companies that have suffered by the actions of others. Even if they have a cause of legal action, the wheels of the court turn so slowly that, by the time a case comes to conclusion, the company may be long gone. Unless the statute of limitations will run out, you should spend your time with the company you run and take action after your immediate work is complete.

And, finally, there is perhaps the most dangerous scenario of all—one that is often found in family business. If there are a number of related owners, they may blame each other for not being "the one" who saw what was happening and didn't stop it. I have seen this situation estrange brothers and destroy a company. And in the case of at least one business with which I am familiar, most of the initial circumstances were beyond their control, but the in-house bickering prevented the owners from doing anything to correct the situation. Now the company is gone as is most of the family relationship.

Be Kind to Yourself

Don't deny that the stress is tough to bear or the work even more difficult now, particularly since it is almost impossible to get any real relaxation. Acknowledging the toll this may be taking on you could be the start to relieving it. Ask others to help and use those you respect as a sounding board. Even if you can't afford to do all the social activities you've done in the past, continue to spend time relaxing with friends and family as a respite from the pressure of work. Take a day off to break the cycle of stress. You need to be strong and creative, and you can't do that if you are completely worn down.

I have been recommending that you continue to communicate with those around you—I have advised that you should not point fingers at everyone else or act in ways to increase the stress of the rest of your staff. This is worth repeating on various levels because the message is that important. Everyone will be looking to you and measuring how you act as an indication of what is likely to happen in the short term.

You will need the help of your employees, you will need the support of your family and friends, and you will need the confidence of your customers and vendors. Withdrawing from them all will get you just the opposite. Not showing any appreciation will get you less than the whole-hearted cooperation you require. It's in your enlightened self-interest to take care in how you treat others and how you interact with them.

PROVIDE LEADERSHIP FOR OTHERS

Leadership is a vital role for any entrepreneur, and in a time of crisis, it becomes even more important. It isn't always easy to take the responsibility and the pressure, but others expect you to be in charge and you will be carefully watched. If you consciously try to be positive, you will receive positive feedback from others, and this can make the whole process easier.

Your first instinct may be to withdraw and avoid all the day-to-day crises that go hand in hand with a troubled business working its way out of difficulty. Perhaps it is lack of work that requires a cut in hours or some temporary layoffs. It may be a serious financial crunch that makes every other incoming call one asking for payment information. No matter how bad it gets, you must be there and do your best to work through the issues with others who work for you. How do you think they would react if the leader jumped ship? Even if you don't have all the answers, seeing you at least working on solutions will motivate your employees to work along with you.

In addition, by making yourself absent, you will be spending time alone without a mission, and that will expand your feelings of isolation. Stay active, stay involved and everyone, including you, will work better.

MEET THE CHALLENGE TO TURN YOUR BUSINESS AROUND

What you have been through and what you are about to face isn't easy. Any turnaround involves tough decisions and hard work. It may take months to see any response, and through it all, not everyone will agree with all your moves. You will be tested along the way.

For those in the early stages of their business career, this can be a challenge and worth the effort for the long haul. You must realize that attempting a turnaround situation requires a commitment beyond that of a typical entrepreneur—you'll have extra work beyond your regular 60-hour week. And all along, your company and your livelihood will be at risk. If you are a true entrepreneur at heart, you are more comfortable with risks than most others, so this may not concern you.

The journey along the way will teach you more about business in general as well as about your own than virtually anything else you've attempted in your business career. What you learn will be of use to you no matter what the outcome for your own company—it certainly has been for me. And if you successfully restructure your business, it will come out stronger than ever before and prepared to face years of challenge ahead. Surviving a crisis prevents you from ever being complacent again.

Recognize When to Sell Your Business

However, if this is late in your career, the work ahead may seem enormous, and you may not be convinced that you want to continue running the company when the worst is over. If that is the case, now may be the time to get out before life becomes more difficult. Now may be the time to put your operation up for sale and let someone else with the time, energy, and capital resources institute the necessary changes. You may even be able to stay on as a consultant to assist with the work but be relieved of the responsibility. Give this some consideration; it may be a positive alternative.

You may be able to sell your company as a going concern and have someone else assume all the liabilities. If the infusion of outside capital could create a valuable opportunity for success, this can be marketed to someone else looking to buy a business. You may be able to walk away from your problems with money in your pocket and perhaps a job also.

Even if the situation is dire, you could try selling the assets for a price equal to any outstanding loans you are liable for personally. You would have to walk away from debts to vendors and that may be painful. However, if you have had enough and can't see yourself putting up with the struggle any more, you aren't without options.

It is also possible to begin a turnaround with the idea that you will review your situation in three or six months and decide at that time how you wish to proceed. If you make progress and still decide to get out, you have created better value for a potential buyer and should reap the benefits. Through it all remember—it's your life, it's your business, and in the end, it's your decision.

SUMMING UP

You need a well-thought-out strategy for an effective turnaround and a positive attitude to make it work. Take the time to analyze your feelings at this time. Ask yourself the following questions:

1. Are you dealing with your own stress?
2. Are you looking for solutions not blame?
3. Have you taken some time off to relieve the burden?
4. Are you exercising a leadership role?
5. Do you know what you want for your own future?
6. Are you still committed to operating the business in the future?

PART THREE

Reengineering Your Business for Efficiency and Profit

CHAPTER

13

Create a Plan: It's Your Road Map to Success

Before roaring off into action, you must plan out the changes you wish to make. If you do them all at one time, you will create chaos and that will serve no one's interest, least of all the business you are working hard to revitalize. You must take data from your analysis and determine a step-by-step strategy to deal with the most pressing problems. The other chapters in Part III will help you address the specific issues you have decided to go after first. The elements of a good game plan are the following:

1. Identify your main goal.
2. Identify the top priorities to meet that goal.
3. Establish your time frame.
4. List each step as you plan to make them.
5. Establish how often progress will be reviewed and by what standard it will be measured.

IDENTIFY THE GOALS FOR YOUR COMPANY

After reviewing the recent operating past of your company, you should have a good idea of what results you would be comfortable with over both the short and the long term. These goals will differ from one company to another: in some cases, it may involve a commitment to growth so that you can sustain your overhead and current debt service, and in others, it may be just the opposite—a plan to cut expenses and pay down debt so that the company can operate profitably at current revenue levels.

Both strategies have been tried in the airline industry with mixed results. US Air has been on the edge of disaster for many years and at one point made a real run at growing out of its problems by acquiring both a southern region carrier (Piedmont) and a western regional carrier (PSA). Neither one was a good fit, and in 1994, US Air remains in trouble, asking for concessions from employees to stay afloat. On the other side of the coin, TWA used a stay in bankruptcy to cut costs and reduce its outstanding debt to emerge a smaller but profitable airline.

Your goals must be clear first to you and then to the others who will be involved in making them happen. If everyone knows where you are trying to go, you can all run in the same direction.

ESTABLISH THREE TOP PRIORITIES TO MEET EACH GOAL

There are several ways to achieve any goal, but since you are the one in charge of this company, it's your job to set the priorities to see the results you expect. Down the road you may want to begin other projects for improvements, but for now, you have to be very specific about what you want to change in your organization and how.

GOAL A For example, if your goal is to pursue the smaller but profitable model, then your three top priorities might be the following:

1. Cut overhead costs across the board.
2. Cut personnel and reduce costs of benefits and perks.
3. Close borderline operations.

GOAL B If you choose to grow bigger and make it a larger pie to cut up, your three top priorities could be the following:

1. Restructure debt to lower monthly costs.
2. Raise prices and reduce cost of products or services.
3. Increase marketing efforts to increase sales.

While some of the steps overlap in these two efforts, they are going in two separate directions. That is why your goal has to be defined to choose the top three priorities to pursue.

I have worked with both methods and find they have good possibilities as well as risks involved. Shrinking a company may make it less vibrant, and eventually there is little left to operate. Growing a business is always a risk because the increased sales may not be there as quickly as you would like. But they are both within reason to pursue, and your chances of success will increase by advance planning.

DECIDE HOW LONG IT WILL TAKE TO COMPLETE YOUR PROGRAM

You must decide how many phases it will take for you to complete your turnaround program and how much time you will allocate to each step. I assume you realize by now that you didn't get to where you are now overnight and you won't get out in a matter of weeks or even months. The first phase of this program, described in the first section, was meant to give you time to accomplish the real efforts of your turnaround.

You can plan on at least a year to see definite results in your operations, but some progress should be evident in three months and certainly a greater portion in six months. You must give this issue thought and decide on the time frame for each phase of your program.

This is the main reason that turnaround consulting tends to bring on long-term engagements. Even when we assume that a project has a short life span, it usually ends up taking months longer than anticipated. Many of the changes seem to be mechanical, but they all involve human participation. People do not act and they certainly do not change overnight. Be patient; prepare for enough leeway to allow for success even if it is slower than you would like.

LIST EACH STEP INVOLVED IN CARRYING OUT YOUR PLAN

Each one of your priorities has a multiple step requirement to complete. Your plan should list the major aspects of these steps and perhaps the interim time frames for each. Perhaps your goal is to restructure debt to reduce costs. With interest rates lower now than they were several years ago, that may make sense for most companies. The task here is not as easy as going into your bank and asking for a consolidation loan as a consumer might do. You may find yourself completing the following steps:

1. Review all outstanding loan documents to determine any payoff fees and loan requirements that prevent pledging of assets.
2. List each loan and each payment required—also include current interest rate.
3. Have a current appraisal done on all assets that will be used to secure any new loan.
4. Do a restated profit and loss projection using any new loan as the debt service—you must show that your operations can sustain any loan payments.

This step and the first three steps are important elements of any loan package, and they must be done *before* you go on to the next step, which is the most important.

5. Meet with a number of bankers as well as agencies such as the SBA or other government agencies that have loan programs to see if you qualify.
6. The last step is to complete paperwork, wait for approval, and close the new loan.

This six-step assignment could take up to six months or more, and with little exception, no step can be completed before the one that precedes. You must come to terms with this and use your plan to think this through in advance.

HOW TO SCHEDULE PROGRESS REVIEW

Early into your turnaround, you will be meeting with advisors and managers very frequently. It is one of the natural responses to the feeling of impending crisis. After the initial pressure is released, the number and frequency of these meetings will subside. Your job is to keep the momentum on track so that all the tasks will get completed by you and by others.

Once you have set priorities and established the steps required by your strategy, you must set up specific times to come together with those involved to review progress, deal with any setbacks, and make sure the goal is still on track.

Going back to the bank loan example, the periodic review could look like the one shown in Figure 13.1.

FIGURE 13.1

Who Is Responsible	Time to Complete
Task 1 Controller with attorney	2 weeks
Task 2 Controller	1 week
Task 3 Owner to hire appraiser	3 weeks
Task 4 Controller, owner, accountant	4 weeks
Loan package should be ready to go in 30 days—schedule meeting.	
Task 5 Owner, accountant	4 weeks
Task 6 Owner, attorney, accountant	4 weeks
Goal is to close new loan in three months.	

Each one of the priorities should have a similar progress review strategy, and the overall goal to be achieved should also have an interim review process and standards of measurement.

If your intention is to grow revenues by 10 percent over the next year, then you should measure your success on a quarterly basis. Be realistic about your goals—the progress will increase over a period of time if you maintain your commitment and attention.

SUMMING UP

A good plan is a critical element of any turnaround. After you have taken the time to analyze where the problems are, create a step-by-step strategy to correct them.

1. Set specific and realistic goals.
2. Identify the primary elements required to meet that goal.
3. Establish a specific time frame for completion.
4. Identify the interim steps involved in the overall plan.
5. Hold regularly scheduled progress meetings and develop standards for review.

CHAPTER

14

How to Cut Cost to the Bone Without Cutting the Muscle

Once you have a plan in place, the time has come to make the changes you have identified as your goal. Perhaps you need to cut expenses to increase profits and allow you to build the cash cushion you need for the long term. As a part of your completed analysis, you should know the areas that are in need of cost containment and should be targeted for streamlining. Now you want to develop a step-by-step operating strategy for effecting the changes.

Step 1: Set a basic budget floor for the department or area in question.

Step 2: Determine the percentage of cuts you wish to achieve.

Step 3: If you feel that you must shave the quality of your product or service, don't do so without a market test.

Step 4: Phase in over a period of time.

Step 5: Sell your ideas to employees before beginning any implementation.

SET UP A COMPREHENSIVE BASIC BUDGET

When you establish a basic budget, it is critical that you include an amount sufficient to meet all the needs of the department or operation covered. If you operate machinery or equipment, you must budget for adequate maintenance and accrue an amount to set aside in case that new equipment is required. Cutting too close to the edge could leave you out of production as a result of one major malfunction.

Travel and entertainment costs are an easy target for a tough budget cut. For many companies, these costs are an absolute sales necessity—customers expect it and your competitors will be out nipping at your heels if your company does not maintain these contacts. In many cases, the loss of business won't be felt initially, and you might feel that you saved money without any effect. The amount of sales expense that should be allocated in any business varies greatly, and the real problem may not be too much or too little budget; instead, it may be that the money isn't spent in the right places. Take the time to create a budget that allows your company through all its sales efforts to keep up a high profile with your clientele.

If you know that your administrative cost is way out of line, don't just storm through and fire every third person to save money. First, you need to determine what work is essential and how many people it takes to accomplish those tasks. What support do they need in terms of equipment and outside services? Put a number to that, and you will find your minimum floor, but it's not the level that you have to reach. Always leave room above minimum service. You will do your cutting on the margins above this operational level. If you get down to the bare minimum, you will leave little in the way of real service and no margin for error. While you don't need ten people doing the work of five, cutting back too far will mean if someone is out or an employee resigns, important work may not get done. Your intention is to be efficient, not at a critical edge with no margin for error.

DETERMINE WHAT PERCENTAGE YOU NEED TO CUT

When you begin a program of serious cost reductions, you should develop a target percentage for the cuts and where you are going to focus for the reduction. You should total the discretionary (nonessential) budgets of each of these areas. Next you will estimate the dollar amount of savings required to improve your bottom line. Then, you determine what percent of these total budgets must be cut to meet this goal. See the example shown in Figure 14.1.

FIGURE 14.1
A SAMPLE WORKSHEET

Areas to Be Cut	Discretionary Budget Amount
Sales	$150,000
Warehouse expense	70,000
Administrative	100,000
Inventory excess	50,000
Outside consultants	30,000
Total budget	$400,000

If you need to save $100,000, then each budget will be reduced by 25 percent, a reduction that should be allocated to nonessential items.

Spreading the cost cuts fairly across departments won't ease the difficulty that managers have when budgets are cut, but it will make others feel that this is a group effort and not a punitive attack. If you have asked for input to develop this formula, the level of cooperation may be greater than you expect. Money-saving ideas could be developed throughout your operation.

KEEP UP THE QUALITY OF YOUR PRODUCT OR SERVICE

When you look for ways to save money, it may be very tempting to cut back on the quality of the products you use or to discontinue those services you have provided free as an incentive to your customers. If you have offered delivery at no cost, you may be taking a great risk to lay off your driver and no longer provide that service. Ask your customers if this is important before you take any action, and make your decision based on their opinions. They are the reason you exist.

Perhaps you can save money by replacing a service that few people appreciate with another incentive. For example, if you pick up and deliver to clients but only a few take advantage of the pickup service, look into the actual cost to you. Each trip may be costing you a fairly substantial portion of the total order. Why not try a dropoff discount—5 percent off if a customer's item is delivered to your place of business. Start off with a voluntary program, and see if you can't change your customers' habits and save money in the process.

A Cautionary Tale

The worst mistake I've ever seen was a doll manufacturer that began in Pittsburgh and was based on the talents of a creative designer. The company grew fairly large (over $5 million) but never fully developed as a profitable venture. A lot of solutions were tried, including major price increases, which dampened some of its market. But the fatal mistake came when a major cost-cutting drive resulted in much of the cosmetic look of the dolls being changed with little thought to the desires of the collectors. Clothing details were fewer and the outfits were less complete, and no extras were included. The company lost much of its luster, the growth reversed, investors lost interest, and without the money to continue, the end came. I am convinced that it didn't have to happen. Their product had a strong and loyal customer base who would have continued to purchase the products even if minor adjustments had been made to the dolls. It was the sudden and major change in quality that shocked retailers and turned off buyers.

If you must make a major change in the operation of your company, test your plans out on customers before institutionalizing the new policies or material. Even Coca-Cola self-inflicted considerable damage with its introduction of the "new" Coke. With a business in transition, any major customer rejection could be fatal.

PHASE IN CHANGE OVER TIME

Whatever area you have identified as the place to begin your overhaul, don't try to institute all the changes with one wave of the wand. The only exception would be personnel cuts. If you are going to shrink the size of employment in any department, do it at one time. Once you have to go back for a second round of layoffs, you leave a very negative message in the minds of other employees. You don't want the company to take on the impression of being in downward free fall.

However, in most other areas, an organized step-by-step inclusion of change is best. If you are cutting costs, particularly if they affect the benefits or perks of your employees, make the changes as of a future date; then, if you find an area of major resistance, you have time to revisit your decision.

If your goal is to reduce the direct costs that reflect in your gross profit margins, you may want to change from current suppliers to low-cost vendors as a way to increase margins. If you have decided to market a new line of merchandise that has a lower cost, bring the new line into your system a few products at a time. This will allow your customers a chance to become familiar with the new products and allow you to measure their approval. Perhaps you will discover that they don't notice the change. If they show resistance, you can go back to your original supplier before you damage any sales. Also, you will have a chance to test your new vendor and find out if they are as dependable as the one you are replacing. You may find that some suppliers have erratic delivery that necessitates higher inventory levels, thereby making the cost benefits turn negative.

Going into this phase of a turnaround, you will have your plan in place with target time frames. You must also realize that the actual outcomes you achieve will seldom be exactly as you have anticipated. Some of your results will be less than expected, and in some cases, they will exceed expectations. Your phased-in approach allows you to monitor your progress and make adjustments along the way to maximize the positive effects of your action.

Another Cautionary Tale

A small chain of clothing stores I frequent experienced some early success and expanded aggressively. Their debt load climbed, and they needed to grow revenue very quickly to maintain this debt service. From attractive well-merchandised stores, they became almost cluttered with an excess of less desirable merchandise meant to generate as much revenue per square foot as possible. It was a turnoff to me and apparently to other customers as well. Almost as quickly as this new strategy began, it started phasing back out. Luckily for the stores, management changed direction before any damage was done and any customers lost.

MOTIVATE YOUR EMPLOYEES TO SUPPORT YOUR CHANGES

The days of autocratic leadership, even in a small business, are virtually over. Most employees are too sophisticated to simply accept the arbitrary decisions of their managers. Managers will not take the word of their boss without any questions. Even if you discourage face-to-face dissent, what goes on behind your back may be even more damaging.

Effective leadership includes the support and motivation of the entire team based on the knowledge that every member makes a contribution. Just as you have included your key employees in the analysis phase and the strategic planning phase, now is the time to continue the process into the implementation phase. In some cases you may have to overrule the recommendations of a manager and make a different decision. That doesn't mean that you should implement by edict. Walk your employees through your decision process, and use your skills of persuasion to explain to them why you came to your own conclusions. Getting everyone on board is the first step in creating successful change.

For those who are involved in the internal operations of your business, if they believe that what you are doing will lead to a better future, your employees will use their efforts to make sure the changes work. Less enthusiasm = less effort = less results.

For your sales and marketing staff, a buy-in is critical. They have the majority of the customer contact, and their dissatisfaction will be translated to clients with negative outcomes.

More Cautionary Tales

The bankruptcy of TWA Airlines was a good example of how to ruin a company instead of change it. Carl Icahn faced down his employees publicly and demanded pay cuts that he said were needed for survival. Even if the premise were factual, the dissension between employer and employee became so great that customers stayed away rather than cross picket lines and feel the brunt of the conflict. The result was a bankruptcy, and the airline that emerged from the proceedings is a shadow of what was once one of America's flag carriers.

The doll company I described earlier in this chapter also neglected to get its sales staff on board for the changes management felt compelled to make. I'm not sure if even a great selling job could have convinced retailers to go along with the production changes, but with a marketing staff that wasn't enthusiastic, there was virtually no chance for acceptance.

Information is power, so the more information you volunteer to your staff, the more likely they are to feel empowered to take charge of their own work and make it a success. The best format for presentation is face to face because it gives the opportunity for clarification. Frequent updates on progress are also recommended.

SUMMING UP

The goal is to return your business to profitability by cutting unnecessary costs. An important consideration is that you do not destroy the valuable qualities of the company by making cuts too quickly or too steep. The following are ways to avoid problems:

1. Create a basic plan that considers all necessary expenditures.
2. Use an across-the-board percentage cut that spreads reductions evenly.
3. Don't make all cuts at once; phase in the program.
4. Don't cut quality or service levels arbitrarily. You want to continue to attract new customers and keep your current clients.
5. Allow your staff the opportunity to participate fully in your program by keeping them involved.

CHAPTER

15

Review the Cost of Personnel, Perks, and Benefits

The most visible expense of your business may be the cost of employees, and it is also a cost you cannot defer. A very common experience for entrepreneurs is the pressure of making a payroll. Anyone who hasn't had the experience of that pressure doesn't really know what it's like to be in business. And it is often in the light of a close call when you are not sure you'll have sufficient funds for payroll that the decision is made to lay off employees. That is neither the time nor the best environment to make these decisions. Instead, the following are several guidelines to follow regarding personnel changes.

- Make your decision based on the job, not the employee.
- Be creative in lowering the overall cost of existing employees.
- Review nondirect employment costs.
- Lead by your own example.
- Encourage and reassure those who remain.
- Be sure of conditions before you increase the size of staff again.

CUT JOBS THAT DON'T CONTRIBUTE TO THE BOTTOM LINE

When times are good, many companies overstaff and keep borderline performers because it's just easier to do so. In fact, this practice may have been one of the reasons you found yourself in difficulty in the first place. Now that you are scrutinizing your employment costs, your review and action must be based on the absolute needs of your company. You still have the responsibility of being a good manager.

Your borderline performers should not be terminated under the cover of a general employee cutback. If a worker is in an unnecessary slot, eliminate the slot. If an important task is being done in a less than satisfactory manner, give the employee the opportunity to improve his or her performance before being replaced by someone else who will be a better worker. Eliminating a slot to excuse dismissing an employee and then reestablishing virtually the same slot again is poor management. Your leadership is under study—exercise effective judgment.

Ask for Volunteers

Before you make your decision, you may want to ask for volunteers who may already have been considering the decision to leave to pursue other interests. Large corporations have used early retirement as a tool of force reduction for many years. You won't have the same resources available to grant severance packages, but there may be people in your organization who would rather go back to school or start their own business or stay at home for a while for personal reasons. While rules for collecting unemployment may prevent you from establishing a formal program, allowing your employees to informally discuss their desires with you while you make your decisions won't violate any formal rules.

HOW TO LOWER THE COSTS OF THE REMAINING WORK FORCE

A few cuts may not be sufficient for your needs. When this becomes the case, you will inevitably continue beyond the initial layoffs. Here is where the strategy becomes tricky because the work attitude of the remaining staff is critically important and particularly fragile. What you decide at this point has to be done with everyone's morale as a major consideration.

If you and your employees can accomplish the work load in less than a full regular workweek, part-time schedules should be considered. But do *not* cut back hours if the work remains the same. This action represents a pay cut without any work cut. While temporary pay reduction may have to be considered, this should be done above board and called, unhappily, a wage concession, not disguised as something else.

Remember that your employees will talk about what is happening to them financially to family, friends, perhaps personal creditors, and unfortunately, sometimes to customers. Depending on the nature of your business, this information may further damage your business and cost more than you save. An appliance store in my city fooled around with employees' wages and one of the more disgruntled ones called the local TV station. That public disclosure disillusioned potential customers, and the store was out of business in less than three months.

Consider Part-Time Schedules

On the other hand, if lower levels of business activity have actually reduced the amount of work to do, putting some of your staff on part-time status may be justified. Again, ask to see if there are any willing candidates first and then do your scheduling with everyone's best interest in mind. Keep in mind that your employees' bills will not go down along with their wages so try to minimize the amount and length of discomfort. When the day comes that business conditions are back to or better than normal, you want enthusiastic and loyal employees back on the job. Your actions will be remembered.

If the work load varies from week to week, find the average and staff up for that need. If extra work comes in, start with overtime before considering outside workers. The occasional use of temporary workers may also work and be cost-effective.

Even if yours is an efficient operation, you will have down time when workers are idle and being paid. One way around that is to subcontract out a part of your work. It may be that even with the profit margin for your vendor, the cost of the work will be less than if you do it yourself. And, in some cases, there is work that is fairly simple or repetitive that can be contracted out to a sheltered workshop. These shops employ the physically challenged and can represent a real savings as well as being of value to others in your community.

HOW TO CUT THE COST OF PERKS AND BENEFITS

In the "good old days," you and your staff may have flown first class, entertained in the best restaurants, and played at the most desirable golf courses. When times are flush, this seems perfectly acceptable. I know, in my day, I lived well as a business owner. Many years ago, an associate opened a new plant in Los Angeles, and I flew out for the big event, arriving from the airport in a limousine. At the time, I didn't bat an eye at the expense. Only a few years later I wished I had the money back.

Trim Travel and Entertainment Expenses

In the early phase of your turnaround activity, you may have stopped a lot of spending and now you must continue the process. What may have been considered as a part of the cost of doing business, such as travel, will have to be scaled back. Look for discount fares, lower-cost hotels, and less lavish entertaining. If local expense has included season tickets to a desirable sporting event or country club outings, it's likely that this practice will have to end or be radically scaled back. You may be able to share your tickets with another business so that you can retain the seats, but the days at the country club on the company tab may be over. Don't stop spending time with clients and associates, just scale back the activities.

Cut Back on Company Cars

Another financial drain is from "company" cars. If you are paying all the expense on cars for yourself and members of your family as well as a few employees, the expense may be very high. If they are not a bona fide business expense, you need to reconsider. The real costs may be in the insurance and upkeep. Review the comprehensive policy you are holding to find out what the charges are for your automobile coverage. You may have to drop some of the cars or share the costs with those who drive them. The bottom line is that it's better for everyone to have a partially subsidized car rather than no car at all.

I was asked to spend two days at a small distribution company to do a financial analysis. I had reviewed financial documents in advance and knew they were in very fragile condition. The owner told me that he and the two other managers hadn't taken any raises in several years, although recently all three had leased new company cars. When I pulled up in front of their door, I was surprised to see that each of these leased cars was a premium foreign model that, in my estimation, the company couldn't afford. I included that fact in my report, but they didn't seem interested in any advice along those lines. They felt that they were entitled.

Examine Health Care, Life Insurance, and Related Compensation Costs

This probably has been one of the fastest-rising costs over the past years and also one of the most volatile from the standpoint of cost sharing and other methods of cost containment. Over recent years, more strikes and work actions have been staged over this concern than virtually any other single issue.

For many companies, the cost of health insurance is high, and the cost of worker's compensation insurance continues to see huge annual increases. It may seem as if there is nothing to do to save money but there are a number of options to explore. Find a good insurance consultant or an agent who is willing to work on a consulting basis. Have them explore various alternatives including employee contributions, higher deductibles, reduction of some benefits, the use of an HMO, joining a larger organization group and participating in their coverage and, if you are large enough, self-insuring your worker's compensation. In all cases, you should make sure that your staff be reasonable with claims and understand the need to keep usage in line. Good practice equals lower premiums.

Save Money by Leasing Employees

There is a new type of employment service that has developed over the past few years that allows you to lease your own employees instead of employing them directly. One of the benefits to you is that you no longer have any of the administrative costs associated with payroll such as producing the checks and tax reports. *And* the overall cost of your benefit package may go down substantially. It's purely a case of economy of scale. With a leasing company having such a large pool of employees, they can negotiate lower rates for the same insurance coverage that you may currently be providing. In some cases, your employees will be able to receive a higher level of coverage. Your working relationship with your employees will not change at all—you still hire, fire, and manage.

DON'T EXEMPT YOURSELF FROM CUTS

If you have been sustaining a high level of personal expense, I hope by now you have succeeded in reducing your own overhead—first, because it will relieve some of your own pressure and, second, because it will make it easier to reduce your own draw from your company.

You *must* participate in any round of cost cutting for a number of reasons, beginning with the fact that the company may no longer be able to afford your previous level of pay and perks. This may not be the case forever, but if you don't cut now, you may never get to forever.

Equally as important is the need for you to show leadership on the issue of belt-tightening. If you are asking your employees to absorb any sort of pay freeze, benefit reductions, or other forms of cuts, then your life-style will probably become of greater interest than ever before. You don't need to make a big issue of your own sacrifice even if it has been major. In very tough times, you may have missed more than a few paychecks. Few of your employees will understand how you may have voluntarily made that decision or how, at times, not only have you not been paid but you have put additional capital into your operation. What they will feel is the pinch of their own sacrifice and want to reassure themselves that everyone including you is participating in the pain. Remember that the cosmetics are important: what type of car you drive, how and when you vacation, and ways you may entertain clients. Lead by example.

Provide an Example for Your Vendors

Finally, you may not be able to pay all your vendors on time and for the full amount. This may include local suppliers and those who know you well. Their perception of what you are doing to cut spending will be formed in part by how they see you change your own personal habits. You may be trying to work out payment agreements and need the patience and indulgence of these vendors. Don't give them the impression that you are maintaining your life-style with the money that you haven't been paying to them. I have seen lawsuits filed primarily out of personal anger. Try to be sensitive to this even if it is based on mistaken assumptions. Be reasonable about yourself and hope that others will share the behavior.

HOW TO ENCOURAGE YOUR REMAINING PERSONNEL

In large corporations where there have been major reductions in employment, personnel managers have identified emotional difficulties in those employees who have remained on the job, based partially on the concern that their existing position is in trouble as well as partially over feeling guilty that others have lost jobs and they have not. The same phenomenon comes into play in a smaller company as well.

With limited personnel resources, it may be difficult to set up the face-to-face meetings and communication system that your employees who remain might need. But you should be aware of what they may be feeling and try to give them a chance to express their thoughts if they want to do that. Don't adopt the attitude that they are lucky to still have their jobs. You all need each other at this time—act like it!

HOW TO KNOW WHEN TO BEGIN HIRING AGAIN

It is often impossible to know exactly what level of business activity to expect next month, much less next year. There are so many variables, some within your control and some not. When your business is in the midst of a major change, the amount of activity can fluctuate from month to month. The decision of how deep to cut personnel is a tough one, and you will probably second-guess yourself several times after the initial cuts are complete. You may see a temporary increase in orders and begin to believe that you better begin to hire again, or it may slow a bit more and you feel as if you should go into another round of cuts. My advice is: "Absent any tangible evidence of a change, don't take any action." The evidence I am describing may take the form of either losing a contract or winning a firm order from a new customer.

You are presiding over a fine balance: keeping the company stable, correcting structural problems to achieve better results, and remaining ready to move forward when the opportunity presents itself. Your employees will be a key ingredient in your future growth; you must keep them interested and involved, yet not feeling overburdened. As the work load begins to grow again, you must be aware of the pressure everyone may be under to continue to meet deadlines and serve your customers. Ask for input and give serious consideration to the opinions of your staff.

Hire with Caution

If business continues to improve, you may want to hire part-time workers before going on to rebuild a larger staff. Several at-will employees who are willing to come in if needed will allow you to meet the market requirements of your product or service in a cost-effective manner. You can hire directly or use the service of a temporary employment agency. There are students and workers with important family responsibilities who prefer the flexibility of permanent part-time work.

Contracting with outside services is a way to increase your output without the cost of employees. Some of the less time-sensitive work you are currently doing in house can be farmed out to other businesses.

As you can probably tell, I believe that the time to begin hiring is after you have exhausted most other ways of getting work done. Full-time employees require costly training and orientation, and if you are experiencing a soft recovery, going through the process of cutting back again is almost too painful to face. Avoid the situation. Keep your staff lean now and in the future. The day may come to rebuild your staff, but be sure of your stability before you begin.

SUMMING UP

The cost of employee perks and benefits can get out of control and must be kept in check. Maintaining reasonable but not excessive employment levels is critical as well. Some of the most effective ways to keep staff levels and costs in line are as follows:

1. Create an organizational chart and staff according to job requirements.
2. Look for ways to reduce costs via use of part-time staff.
3. If times are tough, there's no excuse for the excessive expense of travel, entertainment, and other special advantages.
4. Find alternatives to expensive insurance and keep use in control.
5. Even the owner isn't exempt from sacrifice.
6. Be sensitive of the insecurity remaining employees may feel.
7. If overstaffing has been a problem, don't fall back into the same pattern.

CHAPTER

16

Renegotiate Leases and Loans to Lower Your Debt Service

If your company has been experiencing operational troubles, you may have found yourself driven by debt-service needs rather than the more traditional purposes of business such as serving your customers and making a profit. The monthly panic is about making loan and lease payments, and too much time and energy is devoted to finding the cash to accomplish this because no alternative is explored. I've seen goods and services underpriced and inventory liquidated below cost just to generate sufficient cash flow to meet obligations. If you are in or are close to this situation, now is the time to consider the true implication of this action—you are gutting your business and giving it little or no chance to move forward when the opportunity to do so arrives. There are actions you can take to ease this pressure and you must do so immediately!

HOW TO RENEGOTIATE LEASES

There are a vast number of different types of leases that cover the terms of the monthly payment for the use of property that belongs to others. Some are straight leases and others are lease–purchase agreements. We will review the three major items you may be leasing:

1. Rental property
2. Equipment leasing
3. Vehicle leasing

While all these are legally binding contracts and if enforced, can only be broken by a bankruptcy filing, they can be renegotiated and rewritten if the parties agree. You should remember going into any discussion that you have options to exercise in case of a total impasse. On the other hand, most of these options involve rejecting the balance of the lease and the return of the property. If that's what you desire, a bankruptcy reorganization provides that opportunity.

In cases where you want or you need to retain the possession and use of the items (or property) in question, you will need the voluntary cooperation of the lessor-owner. In changing economic times, you may find the goal of both parties will be to keep a good working relationship even if that means that some terms must be adjusted. The one area where this may be more difficult is with car leases written by the major auto companies' leasing subsidiaries. They are more formal in their rules and will not readily tailor terms to meet a client's changing circumstance. At best, you may be able to get these companies to waive a few months' payments and add them to the end of the lease.

Ask Your Landlord for Help

The 10,000-square-foot building you rented when you started your business or the 50,000-square-foot warehouse you expanded into may now be far more than you need, and the cost may be a burden that is sinking the whole boat. Perhaps you can reduce your space and rewrite your lease for fewer square feet. If you have been a valued long-term tenant, keeping you in the building may be a real incentive to your landlord. Offer a longer term for the new lease as an incentive—for example, if you have one year left and want to rewrite, do it for three to five years. The extra years make it worthwhile.

Another way to ease the current cost of your lease is to rewrite it at a new lower cost in the current year with built-in increases in the future years. The overall result will be an average cost that is equal to your current rate. The temporary decrease given to you now will be paid back over the next two or three years when you can afford it more easily. This has a cost effect on your landlord as he will be lowering his current income, but the benefit will be in keeping some current income rather than the chance of losing all rent. Any willingness to accommodate you will depend on the desirability of the space. But, at least you can ask.

Do You Really Need to Own Your Building?

I have never felt that small businesses should follow large corporations in lock step because they have all the right answers. My own theory is almost the opposite—I believe entrepreneurs are clever, hardworking folks to be admired and emulated. Having said that, from time to time, there are trends that start in the corporate world that make sense. Selling real estate is one of them. Many large companies such as ALCOA and IBM that have made larger staff cuts have also made plans to sell large headquarters buildings.

It may have made sense to you at one time to buy the building you use instead of renting the space. The benefits included a fixed cost and perhaps room to expand. You were also building equity and during times of inflation, that made sense. Now you may be looking for ways to contract. It may be possible to rent out your unused space to another company, but that would make you into a landlord and you will be collecting rents, answering complaints, and doing maintenance for others in the building. You must consider how much of a distraction this would be to your day-to-day work.

Another solution to the issue of too much space is the outright sale of your building. One of the benefits to you that you may not have thought of before is that once you have paid off your mortgage, your relationship with your bank may improve. Many bankers consider their total exposure of loans to a company, including the mortgage, when making decisions about additional loans.

If you want to stay in part of your space, it is possible to sell your building to an investor with a leaseback attached to the deal. A real estate deal that has income in place is very desirable, so a good agent should be able to market a well-priced piece of property effectively. Depending on where you are in your business life, selling off assets such as land and buildings may also be a good move in advance of someday selling the entire company. A business that has real estate as a part of the deal is often harder to sell than one that can be easily moved by the new owner or merged into an existing business.

At one time, I rented space from a toy distributor and I was aware that they turned down a substantial offer on their huge building because they claimed they couldn't find space anywhere else. At the time, they were using less than half the space, and the only reason the cost wasn't destroying them was that all maintenance on the structure was being deferred. Only a few years later, the building and the business started fraying badly, and with little money to fix either, they both deteriorated rapidly. In the end, the business was liquidated and the real estate sold for 30 percent of the earlier offer. If a different decision had been made, at least the company would have had a chance to continue even if it were a smaller operation at a different location.

Rewrite Your Equipment Leases

Of the equipment leases you may have, some may actually be lease–purchase agreements. This means that title remains in the name of the lessor until all the terms of the lease are complete and then one small payment is made by you at the end and the items become the property of your company. Your leases were written on the current interest rate at the time plus a premium that represents the profit to the leasing company. The terms are normally fewer than six years. Many of the leasing companies are small, locally owned operations. They go out and purchase the machine you require exactly as you may have written any specifications. Therefore, it usually isn't in their interest to repossess a piece of equipment that may be specialized for your use and more valuable to you than to anyone else.

You will still have to pay off the total value of the lease, but the term may be negotiable. And if interest rates have gone down since the inception of your lease, you may be able to increase the length of time to pay the balance at a lower rate, and the overall result will be a lower monthly cost.

If you have several pieces of equipment financed by individual leases, explore the possibility of combining them into one lease and, again, extending the total term for the purpose of reducing the monthly cost. In the end, you will be paying out more for the total of the lease, but the value to you now is in lowering your overhead cost.

What to Do About Auto Leases

You may have leased several cars for use by you and your employees and now wonder if you have any options to cut the cost of these leases. While the contracts vary from company to company, there are three different options to consider.

1. TURN IN THE UNWANTED CARS Most leases will require the payment of a termination fee that may be as low as $200. If the car is in good shape, your dealer will be the key to the other charges that may be incurred. It all hinges on the current value of the auto and the remaining payments on the lease. It's worth a trip to the dealer.

2. TRADE IN THE CAR FOR A MORE ECONOMICAL ONE There is a transfer fee involved in this type of deal and also other charges depending on the condition of the vehicle and the remaining time on the lease. If you have been a frequent customer of a dealer and are likely to continue the relationship, here is where you may receive a good cooperation that will lower your costs with minimal penalty.

3. TRANSFER THE LEASE TO A THIRD PARTY If you can find a responsible person to take over your lease, you may be able to transfer the balance to that individual for a very small fee. The only drawback here is that your name will continue on the lease and any default will remain your responsibility. It's a judgment call on your part.

HOW TO RENEGOTIATE YOUR BANK DEBT

You may have a single loan outstanding to the bank payable over a fixed term with a regular monthly payment of principal and interest. If you have a good record of making timely payments, it may be fairly easy to arrange a restructuring of your loan. Stop in to see your branch manager with a firm idea of what sort of new term you will require to allow you to easily meet the monthly cost. Extending the term will mean a lower amount for principal each month. If this isn't a sufficient reduction, try a new approach with interest only for a while and then some regular principal payments and a balloon payment at the end. Even if you don't think that you will be able to come up with the lump-sum balloon at the end, if you have kept up with your obligation, you should be able to restructure that amount when it comes due, over a new term.

Where it gets complicated is when your company has a number of different loans with the same bank and the total debt is high. It is better to start negotiations when all payments are current and your relationship with your banker is a friendly one. Decide how much you can manage on a monthly basis and work with your banker using that number as a goal. If you combine loans and restructure the term, you may be able to substantially lower the total payment. This is not only beneficial to you and your company, but it makes life easier for your banker. Bad loans reflect on the performance of your banker, and he or she has a real interest in keeping your loans up to date. You won't know what's possible unless you try. Your banker may be your best friend in a difficult situation.

You Can Still Negotiate Delinquent Loans

If your business problems have already tarnished your relationship with your banker due to late payments, don't avoid the possibility of setting things right by working together. Perhaps you have gone out of your way to avoid your banker's calls or you no longer go into the bank office yourself to prevent a face-to-face meeting. You won't correct the problems of your business without changing this situation, so now is the time to start.

Arrange a meeting and bring in your current financial records. Discuss your plans to turn around your operations and how long you expect to need extra consideration. If there is a way to bring your accounts current and keep them that way, your banker may be very cooperative.

If your situation has become adversarial with some collection action already beginning to happen, you may need to take your attorney with you or have him or her negotiate in your place. Unless a bank is well secured with liquid (cash) assets, it becomes problematic for them to easily enforce their collection actions. The operative word here is easily.

Once your loans are out of the local office, they become a negative in the record of the manager, so try and catch up with any corrections and renegotiate on the local level. Most banks have workout departments, but their attitudes can vary greatly, ranging from very cooperative to very aggressive, and some have been known to be almost abusive. This is not where you want to be if you can help it. You are no longer a valuable customer here; now you are a delinquent borrower.

If all else fails with your secured lender, the time may have come to file for protection under the bankruptcy laws. The first effect of a Chapter 11 filing is that it stops all collection activity your bank may be effecting even if they have begun taking a portion or all of the proceeds of your lock box. You will then have 120 days to file a plan to pay back your lender, and if you can pay them in full over 6 years, there is a good chance that the plan will be approved. In some circumstances, a bankruptcy allows you to pay back less than the full amount of your loan. You should consult an attorney who specializes in business bankruptcy to see how this may apply to your circumstance. I have also covered much of this material in my earlier book, *Saving Your Business* (Prentice Hall, 1992).

HOW TO RENEGOTIATE WITH YOUR VENDORS

In Part I of this book, I discussed ways to conserve cash, including converting vendor credit into long-term payout. If your suppliers have been going along with this idea and you have lived up to your obligations, then you should be able to continue and perhaps even increase these types of agreements. Asking for extended terms on some purchases is also a way to increase your positive cash flow.

If you must keep the inventory needed to serve your customers over 30 days or buy small quantities of a product frequently, perhaps you can work out a consignment agreement. You will be able to buy in larger quantities and perhaps even get better prices and delivery terms, yet you will be required to pay for merchandise only when it is used. The unused material in your building will actually still be owned by your supplier. The benefit to your vendor is that this type of program locks you in as a customer, and for you, the cash flow benefits are obvious.

There are many times when a vendor only reluctantly agrees to a payout of your existing bills over a period of time. They may need the money for their own business or just plain resent the delay in being paid. In return for the accommodation, you might be asked to pledge an asset as security or to give a personal guarantee. My advice here is against this action unless it is absolutely necessary. Good legal advice is required before you sign an agreement beyond your existing business relationship.

It is always possible to force new terms on landlords, lessors, and lenders, but before you take that route, try to work out your needs directly with the principals. Over the long term, you will find running your operation easier with friendly working relationships still in place.

SUMMING UP

Negotiating for lower interest and longer terms can ease the monthly payments you are required to pay. Some places to look for help are the following:

1. Your rent can be lowered at least temporarily by rewriting your current lease.
2. Equipment lease terms can be renegotiated by extending terms or lowering interest rates.
3. You may be able to surrender some space back to reduce rent.
4. Banks do not want your assets; they want to be paid.
5. Your banker may be willing to work with you—try the cooperative approach.
6. A bankruptcy filing can force a solution on your bank as well as other creditors.
7. Communicate with vendors to work out reasonable payment schedules.

CHAPTER

17

How to Accentuate Your Profitable Business

Every company has certain areas of its business that are more profitable than others. Companies engaged in both the sales and service of a product may actually lose money on the service end of their operation. Or perhaps their vulnerable area is installation. You may have already identified the one phase of your operation that always seems to be a drain on resources rather than a contributor to the bottom line. However, you may be concerned that if you were to make any serious changes, you would jeopardize the entire operation.

This is something I went through in my manufacturing operation. We sold our products to distributors as well as directly to industrial end users, and needless to say, the actual users represented a larger profit margin. In addition, at times some of our distributor customers became almost impossible to satisfy, and their demands disrupted any reasonable production schedules we tried to establish. Every time I came to the point where I was convinced that something had to be done, I agonized over it for weeks before taking action. Even then, when I finally terminated the product in question, or a few times, the customer in question, it was never easy. But with one small exception, the result was positive. We could go back to our desired production schedule or cease inventorying an infrequently used material, and our day-to-day operation became more efficient and therefore more profitable.

DEVELOP AN OPERATIONAL STRATEGY FOR CHANGE

If you have the sense that your company has inconsistent results from its product lines or types of service, then you should work out a plan to correct this problem. The most effective strategy would include the following:

- Do an operational analysis by type of business or type of customer and determine where profits or losses are derived.
- Spend your time, money, and energy on those areas of your business that bring in the best return.
- Consider contracting out the business that shows borderline or no profits.
- You may be able to sell your "questionable" lines of business to someone who can make them profitable.
- If you must terminate a phase of your business, do so over time and help customers to find alternative vendors.
- Promote what your business does well.

HOW TO ANALYZE YOUR PROFIT ON VARIOUS TYPES OF PRODUCTS OR SERVICES

Some companies have very sophisticated costing systems that provide immediate analysis by every product line or service area they perform. Large companies often break down their operations by divisions or business units and then analyze products and services by type. Small businesses usually don't have the systems or the time to accomplish this work. When you are making money from your overall operation, this information may not be important, but if you are struggling, the time has come to decide where the red ink came from and to choose the most profitable direction for your company to take.

If you are the founder of your company, you may have built it to the level it is today by accommodating customers in any way possible. Sometimes the demands of your customers opened up areas of business that turned out to provide high profit and high growth, and other times, you did work to keep busy or because you didn't want a client to go elsewhere. Now, you must determine the impact on your bottom line of those decisions.

Look at your operation as one that makes, sells, or services a number of individual products or customers. Divide the whole into groupings by some common denominator—that is, all "service-only" calls into one category or all sales of one type into a category. Then allocate the direct costs of each. For example, a service call has mainly direct labor cost, your product sale will involve material as well as labor. Each will also carry an allocation of overhead with it. A simple analysis of a service call will look something like that shown in Figure 17.1. A simple analysis of a product sale is shown in Figure 17.2.

FIGURE 17.1
SERVICE COST ANALYSIS

1. We charge $25.00 per hour for service.
2. Our direct labor cost is $12.00 and 40% for benefits for a total of $18.80.
3. Our overhead is 40% of sales—in this case $10.00.
4. We are losing $3.80 an hour on a service call as per this calculation.

4 hours service @ $25.00	$100.00	
Labor cost @ 18.80	75.20	
Gross profit	$ 24.80	
Charge to overhead	40.00	
Loss		($15.20)

FIGURE 17.2
PRODUCT SALE COST ANALYSIS

1. We sell wool suits for $129.00.
2. Our cost of each suit is $65.00 plus $4.00 freight.
3. We pay a 5% commission, in this case $6.45.
4. Our overhead cost is 35% of sales—in this case $45.00.

Our initial calculation would look like this:

Selling price	$129.00	
Less: 5% commission	6.45	
	$122.55	
Cost of goods (and freight)	69.00	
	$ 63.55	
Less: Overhead		45.00
Profit (before tax)		$ 18.55

As shown in Figure 17.2, $18.55 would be our profit on each sale if we were able to sell all the suits at or above their actual cost to us. If any of our inventory sells at less than cost or ends up in our back room unsold, that cuts back on profit.

Don't be shocked by what you learn from this closer look. If you find an area where you are hemorrhaging red ink, you will need to take action to correct the problem. Consider all the implications of the moves—is the service or product actually a draw to customers and once they are in your store, they purchase goods and services from you that carry a healthy profit. If this is the case, then your loss may be in reality an advertising cost rather than a loss.

Your local grocery chain store uses this technique all the time. They advertise a few specials where they actually lose money to attract customers into the store because virtually all of them will purchase a number of other items. Other businesses use the same selling promotion. You can't afford any larger drain of your limited resources so you must know the profit implications of your entire operation.

ADVERTISE, MARKET, AND SELL THE PRODUCTS THAT MAKE THE PROFITS YOU NEED

Attracting customers by advertising low, low prices may be effective for large operations such as grocery stores, but this is likely not the draw you want to use to attract your potential customers. Remember that the message you convey will bring a specific type of client, so go after the ones you really want.

One of my clients operated a small manufacturing operation with a market to both sell and rent their finished products. Outright sales always made money, but rental was far more questionable. All their ads talked about the rental aspect of the business because there was an eager market for the lower-cost one-time use of the linens they fabricated. It was no wonder that more of the overall revenues came in this area, and the drain on the bottom line threatened the entire business. Our work together involved a number of operational issues, but the key one was to convert the customer base into those who were interested in purchasing rather than rental. Slowly we changed the emphasis in all written material from the information on rental to the value of purchase, and we even rearranged the showroom, changing displays to reflect our refocus. Rental prices were no longer posted; they were only available on request. It took six months, but slowly the desired business came and the profits rose accordingly.

The airline industry is a good example of just the opposite pattern. They want the regular full-fare customers who pay a fair price for their ticket, but their message to the public doesn't say that. Most airlines ads you see are those announcing that one carrier's fares are much lower than the competition, most of which fall below the break-even point. The dichotomy is that while these companies really need to attract the more profitable business traveler, most of the time and attention is being spent on the low-fare occasional flyer. It's been a long time since I have looked forward to business travel or felt that I was a valued customer, so I now make as few trips as possible. My attitude reflects the feelings of many other discretionary travelers, and our voluntary abandonment of the market will affect the airlines' bottom line for years to come.

You must learn to go after your best customer, not just anyone who may happen to do business with you from time to time. Advertise to them, call on them, and make them feel valued and needed, because they truly are the key to the future of your company.

You don't want to appear to be completely disinterested in the other customers who are not key accounts because of their small volume or the type of product/service that they purchase. To a new business, all potential customers are important, and you never know if today's occasional buyer may be tomorrow's major account. Nevertheless, your outreach must stay focused on the market you want to serve.

HOW TO PROFIT FROM USING A SUBCONTRACTOR

If there is a product or service that you cannot produce at a profit, that does not mean that another company isn't able to accomplish that feat. A business that specializes in the product or service may be happy to act as your subcontractor, and you both may be able to see profits from the venture.

I am particularly familiar with this situation in the sewn products industry because of my own business experience. Our equipment and production lines could do some work effectively, but for other applications, we never quite learned the tricks to accomplish the required level of expertise. I was often able to purchase finished products from others cheaper than my company could make them ourselves and then resell them at a profit. At times, we purchased the raw material (particularly when we had a good source) and then subcontracted the labor.

Look around at your competitors as well as those in allied industries to see if you can find new vendors that are more cost-effective. Even if the cost advantage is minimal, the value may be that you can focus your valuable time, energy, and resource where the return is higher.

SELL AN UNPROFITABLE PRODUCT LINE TO A COMPETITOR

Before you discontinue a product or service, why not consider selling the business instead? It isn't as far-fetched as it seems. You may have machinery, inventory, a customer list, and history to sell. A competitor who wants to increase its business in this line may be more than willing to buy what you have. The key is in how you present the package.

What you are marketing has a tangible value of assets as well as an additional intangible value to be considered. Your equipment should be priced at fair market value, salable inventory at its current value less a reasonable discount plus the premium value of the sales history (customer use and pricing) and possibly an easily identifiable name or design. If you have advertising material that includes the camera-ready art, this could be included.

Create a letter or flyer describing the business opportunity of the product or service you are trying to market and send it out to the most likely buyer. You don't want to guarantee the profits to be made in this product, but you can be optimistic about the potential that this could bring to a new owner. The fact is that if this market is a better fit for one of your competitors than it is to you, they may be able to capitalize on the opportunity to a substantial degree.

During my 20 years in manufacturing, I was both a buyer and a seller of additional product lines. As a buyer, I found that I could buy dies (steel cutting dies) and patterns plus some raw material at half the cost, and having a ready customer base meant a revenue stream from sales that would start immediately. There is a real value to that aspect.

On the selling side, if my customer base for a product shrank because of plant closings or other market conditions, I could sell off a product line to another manufacturer and realize some cash for the effort. In addition, if I still had sales for the product to customers, I did not want to call my competition; I bought the product from the other manufacturer. In all, it is a better way to sell your excess equipment than by a piecemeal method. This takes time, but it is clearly worth the effort.

LIQUIDATE EXCESS INVENTORY AND EQUIPMENT IN AN ORDERLY FASHION

The time has come to sell off old, hard-to-sell items and put into place policies that will prevent your company from rebuilding its stock of slow movers again. This task can best be accomplished by a good software package that gives point-of-sale information that tracks how long a product has been in stock. Reorders should not be placed on items that have a very slow turn, and if a valued customer wants a special order of an item, you should use all your best efforts to get them to accept the total quantity that you must order to prevent leftovers from being buried in your inventory where they may stay for months if not years. This drain can seriously undermine a company before anyone really notices. Inventory is an asset only if it is current and salable.

When selling off old products, keep this project as separate as you can from your current business. If yours is an industrial business, your inclination may be to give your regular salespeople an extra incentive to move the items, but what you may end up with is distracting them from doing their main job, selling your profitable products. Instead of this method, why not sell your excess items to other distributors in other parts of the country. In some industries, there are services to accomplish this task, or you may even be able to go back to the manufacturer for suggestions on possible buyers. Assign this task to one person in your organization or do it yourself. Since the urgency to find cash has passed, take your time and approach this task logically.

Retailers have another issue to consider when liquidating out-of-date merchandise. Do you want to divert the attention of your customers with racks or shelves of sales merchandise when they come into your place of business. What will be the effect on your operating profits if you drain available dollars from regular sales to below (or break-even) transactions. If you can create other options, you should do so. How about getting together with others in the business area and doing a short-term sidewalk sale? The additional traffic would be of value to all of you. Perhaps you could rent a small space that has been available for a while and open an outlet shop. Again, partner with other merchants and share the cost.

If you have no other choice than to sell your excess in your own store, don't put it out all at once. Keep space in one section as a semi-permanent clearance center and feed inventory into that area over a period of time. Eventually, you will sell most of it without distracting your regular shopper.

Machinery Can Also Be Marketed

Use the same organized approach to the sale of any remaining excess equipment. Research the current value of what you have for sale so you can put a fair price on it. Find all the original information on the specifications and features of the equipment and then create a flyer to send to those you have identified as potential customers. Treat this as a worthwhile sales effort and not as a junk sale. Try new businesses who may still be acquiring equipment as well as out-of-town competitors.

If your plan for the proceeds of your sale is to upgrade your current equipment, why not suggest the possibility of a trade-in to your equipment dealer? Even if they don't do it as a normal course of business, the sale to your company may be an incentive. Most good dealers know where used machinery can be sold so don't be afraid to ask for this additional service as part of your deal.

Intangible Assets Have Tangible Value

As you review the unused assets of your company, don't neglect items such as trademarks, contract rights, licenses, and customer information that may be of value to another company. Have you trademarked a name or patented a design that you no longer use? Do you have a contract or the option on a contract that has an economic benefit even if you are not able to take advantage of it at this time? This could be an open purchase contract for material that has gone up in price or the option to make a future purchase at a below-market price. Have you made an agreement for the likeness or logo of an individual or organization that you are unable to utilize at this time? These are some of the legal rights that may be the property of your company that can be turned into cash. Have your attorney check into the transferability of any of these types of assets you may possess before you make any deals. You may be surprised at what they bring. Several years ago, when the Pittsburgh Steelers were at the height of their success, the rights alone to season tickets sold for over $5,000 a seat. At one time my company had 12 season tickets—a $60,000 asset that I never thought about selling even though I could have utilized the cash more than the seats. Give this some thought yourself—no telling what you will come up with.

Another intangible asset you may have that you probably don't think about is the information you have collected about your customers. In addition to their names and addresses, some of their buying habits may also be a part of your database. Is this information valuable to a company selling other products or services unrelated to your business? If the answer is yes, the next part of the equation is a judgment call. Could you create a marketing list and sell it to an interested company without running the risk of offending your current customers? You would charge per name for this list, and if your database is large enough, this could bring a nice cash bonus.

HOW TO CONTINUE GOOD CUSTOMER SERVICE WHILE TERMINATING A PRODUCT OR SERVICE

Good customer service requires advance notice. If you are unable to sell your product line to another company and are forced to discontinue offering it to customers, don't just take the action abruptly. Consider how you would feel if you had been purchasing material or a product or having a service performed by one company for years and suddenly they were no longer able to provide for your needs. Depending on the level of inconvenience, you may be annoyed enough to make you go elsewhere for your other needs as well. You don't want this to happen to you and neither do your customers appreciate finding themselves with a supplier they had been counting on to meet their requirements. It's good policy to go the extra mile for your customers.

What to Do for Your Customers

1. Notify all customers (or post the information in your place of business) with at least 60 days of warning that items or services will no longer be offered.
2. Sell off your existing inventory at a special price to allow customers to stock up if they want to.
3. Offer an alternative product or service if there is one.
4. For those who request the information, help them find out where they might be able to purchase what they need.
5. At all times, remember that your customer is a valuable asset and treat them accordingly.

HOW TO PROMOTE WHAT YOUR BUSINESS DOES WELL

As years pass, it is easy to deviate from your original business concept. In fact, sometimes it's a wise move to change from the past. One of your important roles is to determine exactly what product or service your company is interested in selling and to be sure this is the way you position yourself through your image and promotion. You may even have to go as far as changing the name of your company to reflect what you want customers to remember about your business. You must know what you do best and make sure others know this information by the image you create.

A number of years ago, U.S. Steel Corporation decided that its name was no longer relevant because less than half its revenue and even less of its profit came from the manufacturing of steel. To reflect a more diversified business, it changed its name to USX Corporation. When United Airlines wanted to be thought of as a complete travel company, not simply an airline, it changed its name to Aegis, but no one liked it and the name was changed again to United Airlines. Does your name describe what your company manufactures or provides? If not, consider a change.

What does your logo or written material say about the major products or services? If you were unfamiliar with your own business, what major message would you receive from the letterhead you use or catalog you send in response to an inquiry? If it isn't completely clear to you, any potential customer is sure to be confused.

There was a time that creating a logo, brochure, or catalog was an expensive proposition. With desktop publishing capabilities, this is no longer the case. You may have someone on your staff who can use the combination of graphic software and clip art to create effective material to tell the real story of your company. If you don't have inhouse capabilities, there are a number of small graphics firms that can do the work in a cost-effective manner. The franchise printing operations can reproduce your brochures, catalogs, or newsletters for pennies per item. As an example, ten years ago, I had an agency create a brochure for my products and the cost was $6,000 with artwork and printing. I recently helped a client complete the same type of marketing material for a cost of less than $1,000. This is the positive effect of modern technology.

Your company has a story to tell—it includes who you are, how you came into being, and what service you provide. For many companies, this is a very interesting story and one that puts a human face on business and creates interest and loyalty among customers. Consider what your story is and make sure that your public image is consistent with those facts. In Part IV, we will cover this topic further.

SUMMING UP

Knowing where the profits are is critical and capitalizing on that knowledge is astute practice. Here are tips to make that happen.

1. Take the time to find out where your company really makes its profit.
2. Contract out products or services that can be done more effectively by others.
3. Sell off product lines to competitors to add to your cash cushion.
4. Liquidate excess inventory or equipment.
5. Don't change gears without warning customers and try to assist them in finding other sources of supply.
6. Create your company image to reflect the business your company wants to attract.
7. Promote yourself by accentuating the positive—tell your story in words and actions.

CHAPTER

18

Develop the Controls to Keep the Company Stable and on Track

Once you have taken energy and effort to restructure your company, the last thing you want to experience is the return of structural problems. A second round would be not only overwhelming to face but extremely difficult to successfully overcome. The bottom line: fix your business once and then take the time to develop a complete set of controls to prevent a relapse into problems. This phase of operational change is critical. There are four main areas to work on to maintain control.

1. Establish a budget procedure for this year and future years.
2. Create an organizational chart; delegate authority.
3. Set standards for the accountability of managers.
4. Write and implement a job description for yourself.

HOW TO ESTABLISH AN EFFECTIVE OPERATIONAL BUDGET

Many small business owners view the process of creating a budget as a boring, time-consuming, and unnecessary chore, but it really can be a creative venture as well as a constructive use of time. And the bottom line: it is an absolute necessity to put in these types of controls, particularly if you have experienced past difficulties.

During a manager review with one of my clients, we discussed what had been our most productive work over the past few months. I was pleased to have the design of a budget included as one of the better achievements. The main reason this task was identified as productive was that everyone felt positive about the process used to construct the document. It was not done by a computer or by one person with a green eyeshade.

An effective budget includes the input of line managers and department supervisors. Even if many expenses cannot be adjusted downward, there are always areas that can sustain less funding by adopting a more cost-conscious orientation. Equally, there are other places where more funds should be allocated to improve the overall effectiveness of the business. These are the decisions that should be made by a group consensus rather than arbitrarily by one individual. If your employees understand that their opinions are valued, they will be likely to implement your budget more effectively.

If you are operating a manufacturing business, equipment repair or replacement is a natural place for discussion. Are you spending more money on a monthly basis just trying to keep old equipment in use when the purchase of a new machine may be more cost efficient? A production supervisor should make this type of decision. Are there ways of cutting administrative costs by using an outside data processing service to produce payroll? Your controller should be making this decision. A budget conference is the place to find consensus of all who may have to develop working strategies based on available finances.

In one of my client companies, virtually no budget was allocated in advance to the sales and marketing category. If an idea came along, money was spent, and no one really knew if the efforts resulted in real sales. In this case, we allocated twice as much money to this category as had been spent the month before and then assigned the sales manager the task of determining how the money would be spent. This had a positive result, as for the first time, this company created a well-thought-out marketing campaign, and sales were generated because of this activity.

A Budget Must Be Flexible

When you begin to create a budget, you will use certain assumptions. These will include projections of your monthly (or annual) revenue as well as estimates of certain costs that you incur in the normal course of your business operation. During the period covered, some of these assumptions may prove to be incorrect, and you must be prepared to adjust your document as you go along so that you can determine the effect of these changes on your overall results. The form that is shown in Figure 18.1 will give you a format to use for a flexible budget. I use this and the other forms, created by one of my associates, Mike Reilly, in my practice.

You will note that in the middle of the page, you can enter the projected assumptions of average monthly figures, and the outside columns allow you to increase or decrease each line item by up to 15 percent. You can change one or a number of items and find out in advance how your bottom line will be impacted. Use this form or one like it to make a budget and review and compare these with actual numbers on a regular basis.

You want to do a side-by-side analysis of your projections and your financials on at least a quarterly basis. If you have seriously over- or underestimated any line items, make the adjustment going forward so you know if your business is performing the way you expect it to far in advance of any problems. You don't want to be blind-sided ever again.

HOW TO CREATE AN ORGANIZATIONAL CHART

The questions of "Who's in charge" can be a source of confusion in many small businesses. Many entrepreneurs overexercise their personal control and run every aspect of the operation regardless whether there are managers in place. Even if this does work in the early stages, as your company grows there won't be enough hours in the day to supervise everything.

The first step in delegating authority to others is the determination of how many areas of your operation will be delineated. Then you list who will be in charge of those areas. Use the format shown in Figure 18.2 to begin the design of your organizational chart. As with other managerial issues, you will want to compile this task with the help of the managers involved from the beginning. The responsibility of the departments will be theirs, and you want them to understand what will be expected. Be willing to listen to and consider the ideas of others.

FIGURE 18.1
FLEXIBLE BUDGET NO. 1

Action Form | **Financial** | **Flexible Budget - 1**

Date: ____________

Flexible Budget

	F	V	-15	-10	-5	Avg Mth	+5	+10	+15	Comments
SALES										
Cost of Goods Sold										
GROSS PROFIT										
Operating Expenses										
Advertising										
Bad Debts										
Commissions										
Depreciation										
Dues & Subs										
Employee Benefits										
Equipment Leases										
Insurance										
Legal & Accounting										
Miscellaneous										
Office Expense										
Other Administrative										
Professional Fees										
Rent										
Repairs & Maint.										
Salaries - All										
Payroll Tax										
Salary Related Expenses										
Selling Expense										
Taxes & License										
Telephone										
Travel & Entertainment										
Utilities										
Vehicles										
Warehouse										
TOTAL OPERATING EXPENSE										
OPERATING PROFIT										

Flexible Budget Action Form - will aid in showing your break even point at various levels of sales/gross profit. The F stands for fixed expenses; V is variable or semi-variable (insert the $ of expense as you see the expense.) Work from the average month either up or down as your sales progress.

FOCUS Group

FIGURE 18.2
ORGANIZATIONAL CHART, OPERATIONS

Action Form | **Operations** | **Organization Chart**

Date: ____________

Organization Chart ______________________

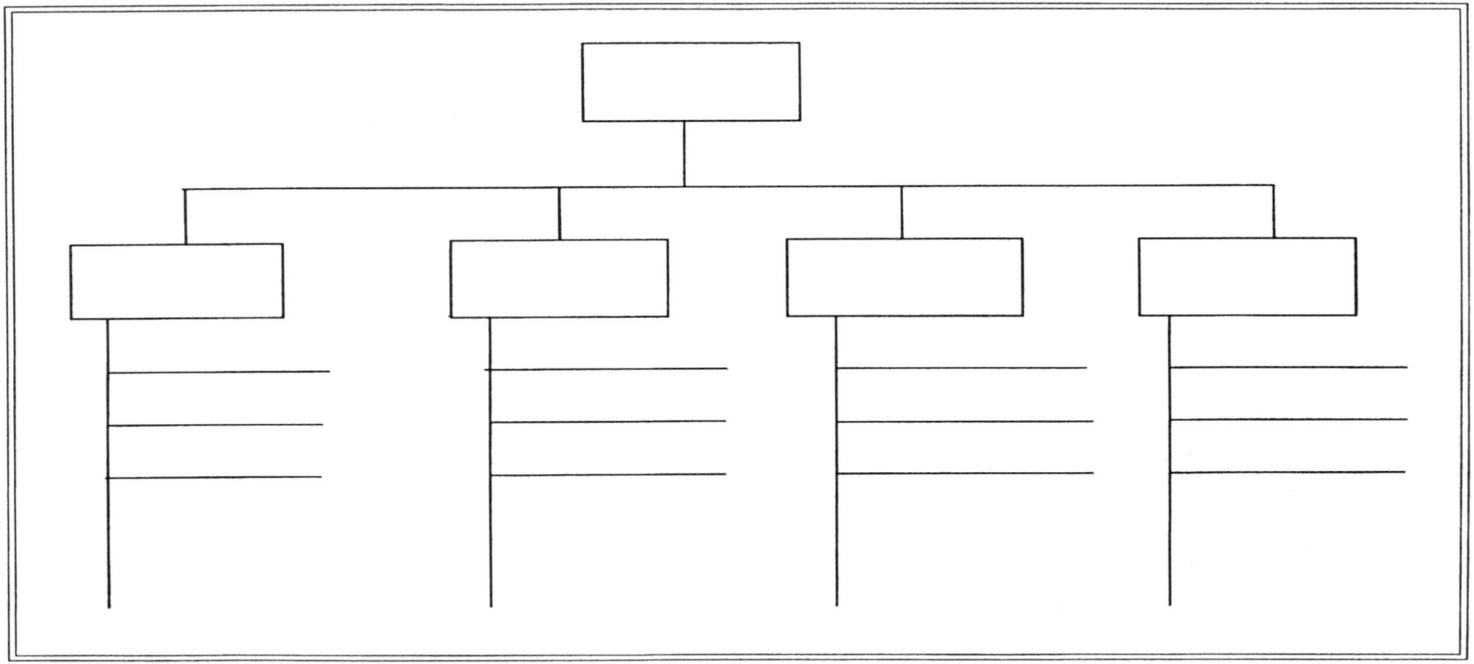

FOCUS Group

After you have created the skeleton of your chart, the next step is to establish various types of authority and responsibility for each area. The job of each manager should be delineated in a full-blown job description document that describes all scopes of responsibility including the ability to hire and fire within their own department. If your managers have been a part of your budgeting procedure, each one of them may now have a discretionary budget authority—that is, an amount of money up to a certain limit that can be expended without additional approval. This money can be for supplies, minor repairs to equipment, or small projects. This cuts down on your administrative costs and perhaps even on your overall expenditure. It's amazing how cheap managers can be about their own budgets; they tend to hoard the money in case of a real need.

Each now-autonomous department should have bottom-line responsibility as well as an incentive for achieving their goals in production, sales, profits, or whatever measure has been determined. It may be a financial reward or some other form of recognition. Make a point of singling out good performance.

The chart in Figure 18.3 requires you to shorten the job description to a few words for each slot. The chart will allow the entire management team to determine their own as well as others' areas of responsibility at a glance. The more your managers take ownership of their own portion of the work load and get credit for their results, the better the overall operation of your company will be.

HOW TO GIVE YOUR MANAGERS STANDARDS OF ACCOUNTABILITY

You may have shouldered too much of the burden of your company's operation over the years, and this may be one of the reasons that you found yourself in difficulty. The work and attention required in a start-up is significantly different from that required of a growing entity. If you haven't learned how to delegate authority, you must begin to let go of areas of responsibility to others within the organization. You cannot be everywhere—you need the eyes, ears, and creative contributions of your managers.

The most difficult phase of this change is how to set up standards of performance (usually based on net results—that is, profits or production goals) and then measure their work on outcomes, not on intervening steps. There is always more than one way to do a task or complete a project and others may not set priorities the same way you

FIGURE 18.3
ORGANIZATIONAL CHART WORK SHEET

Action Form | **Chart B** | **Organization Chart**

Date: ____________

Organizational Chart Work Sheet

Major Areas of Company:

____
____
____
____
____

Area: ____________________________
Responsibility ____________
Authority ____________
Cost Control ____________
Incentive ____________

Area: ____________________________
Responsibility ____________
Authority ____________
Cost Control ____________
Incentive ____________

Area: ____________________________
Responsibility ____________
Authority ____________
Cost Control ____________
Incentive ____________

Area: ____________________________
Responsibility ____________
Authority ____________
Cost Control ____________
Incentive ____________

No two companies have the same organizational chart because of the nature of the businesses and the fact that no two companies are exactly alike. However the chart allows you to determine and evaluate the personnel performing the tasks and to also set targets as regards costs and profit from the major areas of the company.

From the example of the chart below make adjustment to fit your company. Once your settled on the chart, it should be posted and a part of your Operational & Procedural Manual. The chart should also be reviewed as business conditions and personnel change to see that the company is able to work to set goals.

FOCUS Group

would. If you involve yourself along the way, the managers will lose their incentive to persevere to the completion of their work in an effective way. Even if you are feeling compelled to interfere, don't!

What you should be doing is determining a realistic set of standards that each department should be required to reach. It may be the number of products manufactured or the dollar amount of sales or the contribution to profit, but each area of your operation has some way to measure its results. These standards are the responsibility of the managers and the issues for which they should be accountable. Make sure that you both agree that the requirements are fair and in reason and also agree as to how often a review will be held. Then allow the manager to make decisions and do their work. Your job is to choose the right manager, monitor their progress, and take the necessary steps if results are not achieved.

CREATE YOUR OWN JOB DESCRIPTION

The final phase of your change process is to change yourself. Companies slip into crisis more readily if no one is paying attention to a change in circumstance that can become a disaster in the making. Just as you have been responsible for the great success your company has enjoyed, you have responsibility for your downturns as well.

Ask yourself critical questions about what your job at the company really is at this time. Are you spending too much time micromanaging the work of other people? Are you paying enough attention to your customers as well as future trends in your industry? Have you become too busy with outside activity and are you not spending enough of your time on the company? Have you become a caretaker of your company while the business environment around you continues to change?

It is not as easy as most people think to work for yourself and report to no one. This requires a substantial amount of self-discipline and a high degree of organization. The time to begin to work on yourself is now!

List the major functions in your company that must be done by you. Be sure that you do not include tasks that are better accomplished by someone else in the organization. Now take this process one step further and consider what functions (such as marketing or financial analysis) are not assumed by anyone and decide if these are areas that should be covered by you. Your role should be mainly overseeing, leadership, and future planning. You steer the ship—it's important to keep checking the horizon.

The time has come to write a job description for yourself. Determine your daily, weekly, and monthly tasks and create a calendar for your own use. Then go about doing your own job as you would want others to complete theirs. Your goal is to put controls in force that will keep your company on the road to recovery and long-term stability. Don't forget to control yourself as well.

SUMMING UP

Chaos is an open invitation to the forces that can destroy any business regardless of its prior success. The final step in a recovery is to create controls for the future. Several of the areas of concern are the following:

1. Budgets are a device used for planning, review, and control. Create one with the help of your managers and use it to monitor your progress.
2. Delegate authority and create an organizational chart to establish the areas and specific responsibilities of your managers.
3. Develop standards of accountability for your managers and allow them the authority to control their own jobs.
4. Consider the most important aspects of your own role in the company and create a job description for yourself to reflect a defined role.

PART FOUR

Moving Toward a Secure Future

CHAPTER 19

Form New Alliances and Partnerships

In the early days, when you started out in business, you may have been attracted to the role of entrepreneur. Many of us think we want to be our own boss, and we don't see the down side of that scenario until after we've gone through our first real business crisis. As you struggle with how you are going to work yourself out of your serious business difficulties, you may feel isolated and without advisors to discuss many of your most pressing concerns. Once you have had this experience, it is a situation that you don't want to repeat. After your turnaround has begun to take hold, you should consider some new options that bring outside resources into your company. Large corporations explore these joint venture possibilities all the time, and now may be the right time for you to reach out to individuals and other businesses to find areas of mutual benefit.

IDENTIFY POSSIBILITIES FOR NEW ALLIANCES

There are a number of areas to explore as possibilities for both short-term ventures as well as long-term strategic alliances. They may provide financial resources, creative or technical resources, additional physical resources such as space or equipment, or new market resources for your product or service. The following are some of the ways these might be achieved.

1. Take on a new partner by selling a minority share of your company to an individual or another business entity.
2. Share the use of your space or equipment with another venture, perhaps a start-up.
3. Develop a product jointly with another company, an inventor, or a university.
4. Establish a joint marketing effort with a compatible company or with your business community.
5. Participate with another company on a large joint project.
6. Merge with another business, either a larger corporation or one of equal size.

CONSULT A COMPETENT BUSINESS ATTORNEY

I have seen a number of my clients attempt almost all but the last of these suggestions without the legal counsel they needed, and virtually all of them have been burned by the outcome. It goes without saying that your best protection is to select people of honor to become involved with, but you also need a clear joint understanding of your agreement. Later on, this can be a critical factor. Make sure you all have considered all the implications of this alliance and then get it put in a written form. A handshake is friendly, but a contract is necessary.

You should describe the intent as well as the expected outcome of your project and seek the advice of your lawyer. If any assets are going to change hands, you will need an extensive legal document to cover this transaction. If you are sharing the cost, the work, and the profits, a less complicated agreement may be able to cover the deal. Don't dismiss the cynicism of your lawyer by saying that none of the bad outcomes described could possibly happen to you—attorneys have seen all of it before. Consider every caution and perhaps go back and discuss them with your intended partner. You should both agree to put it in writing and have it reviewed by a separate attorney for each side. You are preventing any future misunderstandings.

The money you save by not seeking legal advice may pale in comparison to the expense of time and energy as well as money required to sort out a dispute. All the ambiguities that may be in an informal agreement will be fodder for lawyers to fight over if the plan goes awry.

I say all this with some passion because I am still in the middle of a battle that should have been over a long time ago. I agreed to share space with another company and signed a very informal agreement without any legal advice. Damage occurred to my equipment in that space, and instead of settling the issue of fault and the amount of damage, our lawyers have been arguing over the ambiguous issues that were not clarified by our oversimplified document. I realize now that $100 worth of advice could have spared me thousands of dollars of aggravation. Take my advice—protect yourself.

HOW TO FIND A NEW PARTNER

You may have already decided that the work load is unbearable or that new energy is required or that an infusion of fresh capital is essential. All these problems can be solved by selling off part of your business to someone else. The sale can also be to another company.

The first thing you need to decide is what the goal is of this sale. An individual purchaser can be a new and energetic participant in the day-to-day operations as well as a source of cash. It may be just what you need at this point to give you the impetus to move forward. You must ask yourself if you are willing to give up some authority.

There are a number of good resources for finding the right individual. The first place to look is from within your own circle of business associates. With many corporations cutting back on staff, a number of talented managers have been cut adrift, some of them with lump-sum severance packages. If you put the word out that you are looking, you surely will get inquiries from several interested parties. You may also want to place an ad in the local business newspaper or even the business opportunity section of your daily paper. Use a blind ad with a post office box.

Is there someone who has been calling on your company that you have grown to admire and enjoy? Perhaps you might inquire if they have ever thought of being in an entrepreneurial venture. How about someone who works for the competition but may have bigger ambitions? Think about it—there is a vast pool of people to approach with your offer.

For the cash but not the interference—taking on a company as a partner may be the best solution. Is there a supplier or even customer that could benefit from an investment in your operation? Is there a particularly large customer who may want to have you as a captive supplier? Dupont owns Consolidation Coal, and it owns a general supply company as well. Explore these possibilities for yourself. Make it known that you would consider an investment. You never know who will come forward.

HOW TO FIND A NEW VENTURE TO SHARE YOUR SPACE OR EQUIPMENT

There has been much talk in the business press about how to launch new ventures in business incubators. These involved the use of common space as well as shared services to cut costs and share advice as well. Rather than looking around at a fledgling company in your industry as a source of competition, why not invite them in to share your resources and grow together. A perfect match that I have seen is a graphics designer operating directly out of a printing business. The designer has access to sophisticated technology, and the printer has a source of new customers. Other such compatible combinations are a dressmaker in a retail operation or a wedding planner operating out of a florist shop. Large or small, there are unlimited combinations to consider.

HOW TO DEVELOP A PRODUCT WITH A PARTNER

If one of your material suppliers has been working on a new product, how about forming a venture to develop several new uses for their invention? On a small scale, I have seen a food purveyor team with a grocery store to sell prepared foods to customers. On the technical side, many software developers form joint product development relationships with large hardware manufacturers. That's how much of this industry was formed. Dupont has assisted many small manufacturers working with their material to find new uses.

Look around at all the items you utilize in your business on a regular basis. Is there something that you could develop that would improve another product and bring benefit to both you and the other company that supplies the original product? Approach them with the idea and perhaps a prototype, and you may be able to strike a deal to work on an innovation together that would go directly to the bottom line of both companies.

A number of universities have pursued technical research and secured patents on products or innovations that have commercial use although the inventor may not have the ability to mass produce or market their invention. If this is the type of work you are equipped to handle, contact the engineering or scientific department of your local university and explore the possibilities.

The Federal Government Wants to Be Your Partner—and You Get All the Profits!

Did you know that there are over 100,000 engineers operating 700 federal laboratories, and you can use the results of their $20 billion research—for free!

If you are in the middle of a new project and need technological assistance, you can call the National Technology Transfer Center and find out if there is any current or completed research at any federal lab that could be of help to you. You might be able to license new technology for your own business development or even find a government partner for your research and development project. The cost to you—nothing! Even the call is free—the number is 1-800-678-NTTC.

This center, based in the unlikely town of Wheeling, West Virginia, has 20 technology agents who will make a search of the center's database to find the lab or the expert who is working on your area of interest. They will make the contact with the engineer or scientist and determine whether there are areas of common interest. Then, if it is a good match, the agent will facilitate the contact. It's all there for any business who wants to make the effort.

And remember—it's free!

HOW TO BENEFIT FROM A JOINT MARKETING VENTURE

Is one of your suppliers always involved in major sales and marketing campaigns? Would your customer base appreciate their message and would you be able to increase the exposure they are looking for in the public? Contact them with ideas of how you might use their material or their advertising to the benefit of both of you.

As an example, travel agencies always use the printed material of the airlines, cruise companies, and tour operators they represent. If an agency is working on a large group trip, the major service supplier may be willing to pay part of the advertising expense.

If you sell the products of another company, they may be willing to provide you with printed material to distribute to your customers and absorb part of the cost of a direct mail campaign. If you are participating in a trade fair, you may be able to get your supplier to assign its employees to work your booth. All these efforts will enhance your own.

Shopping malls and smaller neighborhood business districts often get together for joint promotion. Many times these are organized by the mall operator or by the local Chamber of Commerce. If they aren't doing all that you think could be successfully accomplished, there is nothing stopping you from making suggestions or creating some marketing venture with those around you. What brings traffic to one brings it to everyone else as well.

You could team with another business to create a contest where ballots could be acquired in either of your locations. You would share the cost of the prize and the advertising and benefit from the increased interest. For Valentine's Day, one of my clients who owns a very popular restaurant teamed up with a florist and a bed and breakfast inn to run a special "sweetheart" contest. They all benefited from the increased visibility.

HOW TO COMPETE FOR LARGER CONTRACTS

If you have purposely stayed away from large projects because you don't have sufficient resources on your own, perhaps another company of your own size would be willing to co-bid with you. If you both are small operators with low overhead, you may be able to outbid a large competitor with higher costs. You may each do a specific type of work and together provide the full service required by the contract.

The first step is to find someone who would be a good match to your company. Between the two of you there must be sufficient equipment and personnel to do the job that is specified. You must agree on who will be responsible for what expenses and exactly how everything from the paperwork to the physical work will be divided. Also, you must agree on what will happen if any problems develop.

The agreement between you two should be put in writing by an attorney, and you must feel assured that everyone is focusing on the critical issues. You may want to do a practice run together on a small joint contract before taking on any really major work.

This could offer you a good opportunity to grow without taking on any additional debt or exposing your company to risk that would be greater than the potential for benefit. You may find a new partner out of the deal.

HOW TO BENEFIT FROM A MERGER

The joint project venture described may be the first step in a courtship that could result in a merger of your company with another one to form a larger and more stable business. If you can't see your way clear to finding the capital for future expansion and you realize that at your present size, you cannot compete in the market or adequately serve your customer base, now may be the time to consider merging with another company. Together you could have more than sufficient capacity to meet current customer needs and be able to grow to meet your customers' future needs as well. A merger is a form of business marriage, so make sure that you have chosen someone who will be compatible.

Early in your discussion, you will need to exchange confidential business information and to do so comfortably, you should both sign a nondisclosure agreement. See Figure 19.1. This provides for a penalty if either side allows any inside information to be given to any outside third party. You will require legal advice from the beginning to the end of this process. There are attorneys who specialize in this field; find one with experience.

FIGURE 19.1

THE ELEMENTS OF A NONDISCLOSURE (CONFIDENTIAL) AGREEMENT

1. The type of negotiation, such as a joint venture or a merger.
2. The scope of the information to be shared.
3. The agreement of both sides not to disclose or unfairly use any private information.
4. The length of time the agreement is in force.

Do not write your own document, even if you think the issues are simple. Take this information to an attorney and have a formal, customized agreement drawn.

If both you and the other owner expect to work together in the new entity, you will need a high level of cooperation from one another. Take the time in the early stages of your discussions to get to know each other well and decide if you share the same business philosophy and goals for the new mergered entity. Once you have given up your own autonomy, it is impossible to return things to the way they were. Many of these ventures are very successful, but some of them are complete tragedies. You can protect yourself by moving slowly, seeking good legal and financial advice, and anticipating problems before they materialize.

A number of years ago, the Figgie Corporation developed a division called Safety Supply America by buying and merging a number of small industrial safety supply companies into one large business. Some of the original owners did very well on the purchase price as well as employment contracts they negotiated; others did not. If you have been approached by a larger corporation in this manner, go to see the best law firm in your area on these matters. The advice you get will be worth the price.

SUMMING UP

New blood and fresh capital may be just the shot in the arm that your business needs to prosper for many years to come. Your co-venture with new people and other organizations can be structured in a variety of ways. Consider some of the following possibilities:

1. Form a new partnership with an individual or another business.
2. Share space and equipment, perhaps with a new venture.
3. Develop a product with a supplier, manufacturer, or university.
4. Launch a joint marketing venture with a vendor, your local business community or other companies.
5. Co-bid on a large project with another small business in your industry.
6. Merge with a similar company or become a part of a larger corporation.

Before making any new commitments, seek legal advice and review all considerations.

CHAPTER

20

Write a New Plan for the Future

Every time I mention the need for a business plan to one of my clients, I watch their eyes glaze over. While every business book talks about the need for such a document, few entrepreneurs know how to write one, and fewer believe in the value of this exercise. Now it's my job to convince you that this is a project that is worth your time and effort.

The longer I am engaged in the practice of turnaround consulting, the more convinced I am that a written plan is an important business instrument. When I work with start-up business, their need to have a plan is primarily for financing sources who always ask for the document. Few professionals ask an experienced business owner if they have a written plan, although I could save hours of my time and hundreds of my clients' dollars if I had a document to review. At least I would be able to see what the original goals and strategies were, and then I could determine where they went astray.

HOW YOUR BUSINESS PLAN CAN HELP REBUILD THE COMPANY

Going forward for you, recording the goals and strategies of your existing business has two primary uses. The first is that you will have a chance to think through all the current issues of your business. You will be required to give this project your full attention, and this is an exercise that has real value to your own level of understanding. As you go back to review your writing for a final draft, you may discover areas that you haven't fully explored or analyzed, and this should motivate you to complete your task of oversight. A periodic review of this plan encourages you to measure progress and make changes before critical mistakes are made.

The second reason to create a new business plan may be more of a motivator to you than the first. Along the way as you are working your way out of difficulty, you may have been avoiding your banker. It is hoped that you haven't damaged what had been a good working relationship, but you probably have had less contact because you haven't been looking for any new money. This will begin to change as you return to show profits and want to fund new growth. A new business plan that covers where you've been and where you're going along with good projections will go far in restoring your credibility as a competent business operator. Bankers need paper for their files, and most of them respect an entrepreneur who seems to have good control of their operation. I have seen this theory in practice and my client was delighted by the response of his banker to receiving and reviewing his new business plan. It wasn't a professional document, but it was well thought out and neatly presented. It filled in the blanks for the banker as to what the company had been through and proved that the owner knew how to face problems and solve them.

WRITING YOUR BUSINESS PLAN

Use a format similar to any plan you may have written before with a few additions. Be sure to include the following

- A description of the existing company
- A brief history of the business
- Your current operating strategy

- Your future potential
- Sources of revenue
- A pro forma financial statement
- Additional supporting material

How to Describe Your Company and Its Mission

The first section of your plan will involve a description of the product or service that your company provides. You will want to begin with an explanation of how the company became involved in its current business; for example, your grandfather was an early furniture maker and the business has now become a retail interior decorating establishment. Or it may be that after 20 years of working as the manager for a large construction company, you decided to become a contractor on your own to do a specialized type of work. What you want to accomplish here is to explain to the reader why you believe a company such as yours is in a good position to continue to be successful in the market with your product or service.

If you have a unique service or own the patent on a product, this is the place you want to include that information. If you are currently working on an innovation to a product, without giving away your trade secrets, you should let the reader know that there is something special in the works. Sell the concept of your company—after all, you believe in it enough to have nursed it back to good health.

What to Include in Your Company History

You want to describe the beginning of the business (or in some cases, the beginning of your leadership) and discuss how the company made progress. Don't shy away from an explanation of the difficulties you have encountered recently. You will have the chance to show that you understand, in detail, what went wrong and why it happened. This gives the reader the impression that you have control of your operation. Every business goes through transitions; it won't shock anyone.

You should go over, in as much detail as you are comfortable with, the steps you have taken to correct any problems you uncovered. You want to point out the progress that has been made in analyzing operations, changing policies and strategies, and creating controls for the future. If you are still incorporating changes, describe where you are in the process and what your ultimate goals will achieve. If you can quantify this progress, do so such as "profits have improved by 20 percent and we expect them to go up another 10 percent" or "overhead has been reduced by 10 percent and the purchase of a new machine will double that number." Your business life is a journey—describe where you are.

How to Describe Your Operating Strategy

You want to demonstrate in this section that you are aware of the changes going on in the industry that you serve. They may be changes in product or in methods of distribution or in customer buying patterns. Everyone is aware of how a business can be blind-sided by changes that they didn't see coming and particularly if this is what happened to you in the past, you want to show that you are now prepared to face the future.

You may even take time in this section to conjecture about the far-off future and describe how a new market niche could open up and your plans to be the first to serve it. For yourself as well as for your reader, you must show that you are not so distracted by your day-to-day duties that you are not keeping one eye on the next year and the many successful ones you hope to come after that.

Describe How This Strategy Will Create Future Potential

You may have been positioning yourself for a new product still under development or a new service that is now coming into demand. This is the section where you create the vision for your company based on this emerging market. Have you formed a venture with someone else that will result in a market innovation? Are you involved in an research and development project that will bring new business to your company over the next few years?

You also want to put into writing your own understanding of where future trends are taking your industry in general and your company in particular. Thinking this issue through completely to write about it is a good exercise for you, and a well-developed strategy for the future will impress your reader that you can make it happen. You want to move the perception of your company from the problems of the past to the potential of your future.

This is a good opportunity to create a roadmap for your company to follow. Parts of this section of your business plan can be condensed to create a mission statement that you want to share with your employees. Every business has a reason for its existence—the product or service that it was organized to provide. Everyone who works at your company should be aware of what purpose your business serves and exactly how you would describe that purpose in detail. You want your customers to have an accurate impression of your business; that starts with the assumptions of your employees.

Describe Your Sources of Revenue

At this point you make the connection between the product/service your company provides and the customers who will be interested in purchasing your goods. You must have learned over the years that these relationships do not remain stable and over time, the type of products and services you provide change and your customer base does as well.

For example, over the past decade, virtually every major basic industry in this country, beginning with steel and auto, has gone through periods of consolidation. Each round ends with a smaller overall industry and, consequently, less sales opportunity for the vendors that serve these industries. If you are among these suppliers, projecting revenue increases from selling the same products to a shrinking market isn't convincing and most likely won't happen.

Therefore, part of the purpose of this section is for you to walk through the validity of your own strategy for the future. You must quantify in numbers how much dollar demand there will be for the product/service of your company and where that demand will come from in terms of individuals or other companies who buy from you. If you are convinced that the revenue source will be there, complete this section because you will likely be able to convince the reader as well.

How to Create a Pro Forma Statement

The final phase of your plan is a projection of revenue, expense, and profit for the next three years. This is always a challenging type of projection, but you may never be in a better position to complete this phase accurately than you are at this point.

First, you have actual business history to rely on. You have reviewed all your expenses and created a budget to follow to keep them in control. And now you have determined where your revenue sources are coming from and you can project what levels your future revenues should reach.

Using these studied predictions, you will create three years' worth of statements assuming that you closely reach your goals. For year 1 you may want to do this on a monthly basis and thereafter on a quarterly basis.

If you can make a convincing case that you will be profitable and have positive cash flow, this may be the time to see your bank to talk about future financing needs. I can almost guarantee that you will impress your banker by the efforts.

What Additional Material to Include

You can fill out your plan by including any substantiating documents that may be available. If you have entered into any joint agreement with another company, this may be added. Demographic research that backs up your predictions of trends can be important. The catalog or advertising copy that your company creates should be copied and included in your plan.

If your company has been involved in any high-profile activities, press clippings are an interesting addition. In essence, any material that breathes life into this dry document will wrap up the package into a more interesting read and more effective instrument. Show that you believe in the viability of your company, and you will convince the people who may be important to that effort.

PLAN YOUR WORK AND WORK YOUR PLAN

This piece of wisdom should become a driving force in your work life. Most entrepreneurs are attracted by the freedom and creativity of a venture of their own. There is a certain amount of energy created by the organized chaos most of us operate under. The effectiveness of these work habits decrease over the life of your business and now is an opportune time to sharpen your focus and develop a more organized approach to your business operation. You will be pleased by the stable results you can achieve by developing a plan of action in advance and using it as a guide to take you where you want to go.

Show your document to your outside advisors (some of them may have seen it along the way) and also to your key employees. Ask for any suggestions and incorporate outside thoughts into the final draft. Then use it and revise it along the way.

SUMMING UP

To better organize your business moving forward from this point and to provide a stable platform for the future, a business plan is an important tool to create and use. Be sure that you cover all the aspects of your business honestly using the following elements as a guide:

1. What is the mission of your company?
2. Where have you been in terms of growth, profitability, problems discovered, and problems solved?
3. What is your strategy to reach your customer and sell your products/services?
4. What is the likely potential for your company over the next few years and beyond?
5. What will be your sources of revenue?
6. Can you quantify your projections in operation statements?
7. Is there supporting evidence or examples of your company's position and strategy?

CHAPTER 21

How to Plan for Your Successor

It is not unusual for an entrepreneur who has successfully steered through shark-filled waters to begin to think about the day he or she may leave the business. Even if you felt committed enough to continue on through the struggle, once you've turned the corner and the adrenalin isn't high enough to meet the challenge, you may want to reassess your own future as well as your business.

Over the years, I have watched the progress of a number of major turnarounds and bankruptcy reorganizations. Very often, the manager who led the restructuring will leave when it is over. Carl Icahn left TWA as did the CEO of Continental Airlines and the chairman of Macy's. It is likely that the combination of burnout and boredom kicked in and these leaders felt that they had no more new ideas to contribute. Fortunately or unfortunately, depending on your perspective, an entrepreneur can't quit and leave his own company. We have to stick with it and decide how to dispose of the business assets. Now may be the time for you to give consideration to this aspect of your life.

Even if you see this possibility as being down the road a few years, it isn't too soon to decide how you will make your exit. A successful departure takes a substantial amount of preplanning. The first step is to decide what form of escape you will take and then to work out the details of the transition. Here are five alternatives to consider.

1. Select a family member to take over the operation.
2. Sell the business to one or a group of insiders.
3. Sell the business or the assets to another company.
4. Sell the business to an individual.
5. Close the business in an orderly fashion and liquidate the assets.

Each of these strategies offers a number of advantages and some areas of potential difficulty, but they all will work better if you take the time to develop a strategy and put it into action.

HOW TO GROOM A FAMILY MEMBER FOR SUCCESSION

This topic is certainly too big for a section of a chapter and likely bigger than an entire chapter, so perhaps I should say, "How to begin to groom a family member." You may already have a son, daughter, or brother working in your company and you assume that if something happens to you, they will take over. That is insufficient planning for the future of your business as well as your own ability to find a way to retire. And it would be a trauma to your successor to find themselves suddenly at the helm of the business. This is something I have experienced firsthand when I took over a family manufacturing company four days after my father's death. How many times I wished that he had prepared me for that job!

What you need to do is sit down with the person you have identified as the next CEO and ask them if that is how they see themselves. You may find that they love working with you but have no interest in following in your footsteps. Get clear on this issue from the beginning.

After you have come to an understanding that you have found the heir apparent, the two of you should plan out the timing of this change of leadership and what you should be doing to train in the interim. If he or she has not been attending meetings with you, now that should change. Your successor should meet and begin working with your lawyer, accountant, and banker. Let people who need to know that you have made this decision and expect to implement it over a fixed period of time. Perhaps after a time, you should begin to pull back and let your successor run the company while you take extended time off.

How Will You Be Paid for the Business?

Succession in a family-owned firm is often difficult because the one with the money is the seller, not the buyer. If you aren't concerned about liquidating your equity, that won't be a problem, but you may need some of the capital for your retirement. Perhaps your buyer may be able to borrow against his interest in the company for a down payment and then pay you on a regular basis until you have been paid in full.

There are a variety of financing alternatives, but I strongly advise that you negotiate this issue on a businesslike basis with the use of accountants for tax planning and attorneys to commit it to legal agreement. Having a casual arrangement can not only cause you not to get the money you expect, but it can cause painful and destructive family misunderstandings.

HOW TO SELL YOUR COMPANY TO KEY EMPLOYEES

There may be a manager working for you who would be both interested in and well equipped to buy your business. Perhaps you have even discussed this possibility when they came to work for the company. If a deal is possible, you may want to negotiate a buy–sell agreement and begin to form a plan to turn over the reins. If you are willing to sell shares over a long period of time (over three years), you may be able to start off with an amount of stock that will provide a minority interest, and after a certain amount of time has passed, the balance of the stock will be sold in one block. This process will ease the financial requirements and allow the transition to be smooth. Again, my admonitions about carefully constructing an agreement that protects both of you. A value of the business will have to be established in the beginning. If the two of you work hard and well together and the company increases in value as a result, this will accrue to the new owner. However, in terms of goodwill and the chance to see your creation go on, it is certainly worth it.

You could sell the company to your employees through an ESOP (Employee Stock Option Plan) where a trust is created in the name of your employees and your stock is purchased by the trust. A company would have to be of big enough size and high enough value to justify what could be a complicated and costly legal transaction.

HOW TO SELL THE BUSINESS TO ANOTHER COMPANY

You must do a lot of preliminary work to successfully sell your business as a going concern to another company. To get full value for the business, first determine how much of a recovery you still need to make and then continue the turnaround strategy until the business is showing the results of your work. The same business can bring a substantially higher selling price if it is groomed for the sale first. A year of work on your company could be more than worth your while. Look at your operation from the perspective of a buyer and decide which areas need work. Perhaps the physical operation has become run down and some serious cleaning and a paint job might work wonders. Keep on paying down debt to clean up your balance sheet as well. Old equipment should be repaired and cleaned—some may need to be replaced. You want a buyer to be attracted to the business—and how it looks, how it feels, and how it operates will tell your story. It should read like a story of growth and profits—a desirable addition to any other organization.

The question of what to tell your employees is a bit tricky. The fact that you are doing work may make them concerned about your intentions. If they begin to see interested prospects walking through, the word is bound to spread. What you don't want is for valued employees to jump ship as the process is proceeding. If you don't sell the company quickly, you'll have to run it without them, and the value of the business itself will go down.

If you sell to a larger corporation, you may want to get an outside lawyer or consultant to negotiate for you. This will allow you to take extra time to consider any offer as your advisor will bring it back to you. They can make higher demands than you because the buyers expect that of a professional you hire and you may be surprised at the deal that can be made. If a large company is interested in you, it has identified something about your operation that interests management and may be willing to pay a premium for it.

Selling to a company your own size or even smaller may be a more casual event. You will probably be required to set a price and then find out if the other side has sufficient capital to make the deal. If your two companies are a good fit, a bank may be willing to finance the purchase because of the potential of a combined operation.

The Nondisclosure Document

In Chapter 19, I mentioned a nondisclosure document, and this is a critical aspect of your selling process. At some point in your negotiation, you will share confidential financial information and at least some of your customer data as well. You want to assure yourself that the confidential nature of this information will be respected, and a nondisclosure document offers some protection.

Consider Flexible Financial Terms

Structuring a deal with a smaller company may require flexible financial terms. You may be paid out over a period of time instead of all at once. It goes without saying that this type of deal can be risky, and if this represents money you will absolutely need, it may be a risk you can't afford to take. If the down payment is high enough, that may take away some of the sting if the rest of the deal doesn't pan out. You also may be able to write a sales agreement that requires any failure to pay to result in the forfeiture of the business back to you. Then you can sell it again.

HOW TO FIND AN INDIVIDUAL TO BUY YOUR COMPANY

The various ways I described in Chapter 19 to find a partner are also good ways to find an individual to buy your company outright. Someone working for a company in your industry or an early retiree with some ambition and capital to invest are good candidates. You can also put the word out in your business network, with your lawyer, accountant, and banker. These professionals will often know of individuals looking to start a business and for many would-be entrepreneurs, buying an existing company is a better bet. Most start-ups turn out to be more difficult than the founder anticipates, so you can market the value of a going concern—one that already has a customer base and a revenue stream.

If your business has any special potential for a minority or woman entrepreneur, seek out organizations that train or make loans to nontraditional business owners and let them know that you have a company to sell. You may be providing a special opportunity for a deserving individual and you can take pride in the future of your creation. There can be special funding set aside for minorities that will allow you to be paid in full.

Create the effort around selling your business the same way you would sell your products. You may want to write a brochure describing the features of the company and the current achievements as well as the potential for the future. Sell the same challenge that attracted you.

Consider Hiring a Business Broker

You may find the whole process easier and more effective if you turn the sale of your business over to a broker. They will advise you about what you need to do to make the company more desirable, and they will advertise and market the business. Needless to say, brokers charge a commission on the sale of the company, and some may charge an upfront fee as well. This will depend on the amount of work involved in preparing for the sale, perhaps including setting a price by analyzing the current value of your company. A consultant's fee is often standard practice for business brokers, so you should call more than one and ask about how they charge before making your decision.

HOW TO CONDUCT AN ORDERLY SALE OF YOUR ASSETS

It may be that you feel that the market for your product or service is diminishing and your business would be very difficult to sell. The longer your company is on the market, the more the business may slow down as customers look elsewhere if they know that ownership is changing hands. As all this is happening, the value of your equity is slowly ebbing away. While this is a difficult reality to face, perhaps you must do so and take steps to sell assets when they still exceed liabilities.

This decision is often made when a lease comes up for renewal. It doesn't make any sense to go on for three or five more years, and now is the time for an orderly liquidation. You may be able to sell all your inventory and equipment and pay your bills and pocket the difference. Don't forget that you may have customer information to sell to another company.

There are a number of liquidators or auctioneers that you could call in to conduct your final sale. If you have inventory, a liquidation will often bring in additional merchandise to spice up the sale. Machinery and equipment may do better at an auction. Plan any sale well in advance, and your results will be increased by this work.

You will have to settle the secured (bank) debt of your business as well as any outstanding taxes before you can close the books on your company. However, if you are running an incorporated business, you will not be held personally liable for any unsecured debt that would be primarily vendor credit. I'm not recommending that you do this, but if you find yourself in the position of not having sufficient funds to take care of all bills, you can lock the door and walk away. I recently saw a franchisee of a hot restaurant chain do just that—even though he is a lawyer and operates other franchises separately incorporated.

If you have been in a business for a long time and have a customer following, consider taking these relationships and going to work for a former competitor. Even if you want a change, spending the time to create additional sales for another company could result in an income stream of commission for a while to back you up financially as you pursue other interests.

SUMMING UP

The time will come that you want to cut back your work or perhaps even leave completely to live a life of leisure. The ease with which you accomplish this phase of your business life will be directly impacted by the time you spend to plan your exit. Here's a checklist of things to consider in your plan.

1. Is there a family member who is ready, willing, and able to take over the company?
2. Can you take out enough of your personal capital to fund your retirement or change of interest?

3. Are there employees of your company who might be interested in a buy-out?
4. Are there sufficient assets to justify setting up an ESOP?
5. Is there another company that would benefit from acquiring your business?
6. Do you need a business broker to market your company?
7. Have you made your attorney, accountant, and CPA aware of your interest in selling out?
8. If you feel that your business can't be sold as a going concern, have you thought about conducting an orderly liquidation of your assets?
9. Are you taking action before action takes you?

CHAPTER

22

Going Forward with the Business of Business

You may feel as if you've been under relentless pressure for a long period of time, and you probably are right about that. Once the work has been pretty much complete and the turnaround put in place, it is easy to experience a letdown and sense of bone-numbing fatigue. My next piece of advice may be one you'll really like—now is the time to take a vacation! Get away from your work and play at whatever interests you the most. At this point in our work, one of my clients looked at me and said, "I know you won't approve of this, but I want to get away and play some golf." To his surprise, I ordered him to go—after the stress he had endured, this trip was an absolute necessity. We still had work to complete, but it could wait.

If you are to sustain your interest in continuing with your business, you will want to go back to the normal day-to-day activities that you did early in your career and, it is hoped, you enjoyed. To feel comfortable in getting back into that mode, you will need closure on the turnaround process. I recommend the following three-step strategy in moving on to the work that you set out to do.

1. Report the effort and its result to all the stakeholders in your company.
2. Relaunch the business with a new look and new attitude.
3. Take time to periodically check the pulse of your business to make sure it doesn't slide back into trouble.

HOW TO REPORT AND TO WHOM

If you do not know who the stakeholders are in your company, just consider all the various constituencies who are affected by the well-being of your operation. For most companies, this list would include the following:

- Investors
- Employees
- Lenders
- Vendors
- Customers
- Landlords
- Professional advisors

Your list may be even longer than this one.

Each of these groups will have known about your difficulty and have been impacted in one way or another. Some of them may have lost money over the situation, and even those you paid in full may have waited longer than they would have liked to receive payment. You may have been communicating with many of these people or organizations on a regular basis, but it is not unusual for the frequency of your communication to tail off after a period of time. You don't want to be thought of forever as a business in trouble, and the way to put a stop to that perception is through information you release. It is in your own interest to complete this task.

Send Out Your New Business Plan

This document should be delivered to your banker along with a cover letter and an offer from you to discuss it further if he or she wishes to do so. You should make an appointment to stop by for a short chat and then allow the banker a chance to read over the material after you've gone. Check back in a week or two to see if there are any questions. Your open communication will be reassuring to your banker as will the document you leave behind. All this transmits the clear message that you have conquered your problems and are ready to go on about your business. In some ways, really good bankers are even more inclined to make loans to your company because they know that when the going gets tough, you hang in there and see it through.

The other natural recipient of your new business plan would be anyone who has invested in the business and may have been at risk during the turnaround. Share the results of your work and your projections of the future with those who will appreciate it. Also in this category would be your professional advisors such as accountants, lawyers, and yes, even consultants who may have helped with part of the work. It's an opportunity for you to receive some compliments on your efforts and allows those who were a part of the struggle to feel good about the outcome.

Speak to Your Landlord in Person

It is possible that your landlord may have wondered how long he would have a tenant and be quietly looking for someone else to move into your space. You need to make clear that you expect to be around for a while and will be a secure tenant for years to come. The last thing you need is to come to the end of your lease and find out you won't be offered a new one. This is a potential problem that can be solved before it happens.

Speak to Your Employees

Even if you have been updating your employees over the entire period of your turnaround efforts, they need to hear directly from you that the danger has passed, employment is now secure, and the company has a plan for the future. Depending on the nature of your employees and the current level of your finances, now may be the time to have a social event and let everyone blow off a little steam. In addition, it is a way to thank them for their effort during difficult times. Your remarks needn't be extensive. It should be sufficient to acknowledge that the business problems you had been struggling with had been in great part overcome due to the contribution of everyone. Further, you want to identify the steps that have been taken to move forward and encourage everyone in attendance to share future growth and prosperity. The goodwill you can generate by an event such as this may make it well worth the cost.

Write a Letter to Your Vendors

At this time you want to redirect the image of your company from where it had been among suppliers and to put your competitors on notice that you are back stronger than ever and ready to give them a run for their money. A simple but direct letter to your vendors could begin that change in perception. People talk (men as well as women) and what you say in your letter will get out and make the rounds. Figure 22.1 is a sample letter that you may change to meet the specifics of your own situation.

FIGURE 22.1

September XX, 1994

CEO

ABC Corporation

Dear Supplier:

Over the past 15 months, we have been engaged in a major restructuring of our business operation. As you know, we closed one production line and consolidated our administrative operations. There were times during this period that our payments to suppliers were delayed. We want you to know that we sincerely appreciate your cooperation during these periods.

With our new sharper focus on our core business and our increased marketing programs, we look forward to an exciting future. We hope to continue working with your company to our mutual benefit.

Again, our thanks for your assistance and we welcome any questions you may have.

Sincerely,

XYZ Company

You Should Also Write to Customers

Some of your customers have known about your restructuring, and some may not even have thought about it. Don't be surprised, however, if your competition has circulated as much information as they could to get an edge on your company. In fact, it wouldn't be unheard of to find out that rumors were spread that exaggerated your situation. Now it is your turn to blow your own horn, and you want to do so in a way that will make everyone feel secure about the future of your business. Figure 22.2 is a sample letter you might send to your customers.

FIGURE 22.2

September XX, 1994

ABC Company

ATTN: Mr. A

Dear Mr. A:

The XYZ Corporation is always interested in discovering methods to make our operation more efficient to give our customers the best service at a competitive price. Over the past 15 months we have undergone some major restructuring to meet those goals.

If there was any interruption in our service to you during this time, we apologize. We welcome your inquiries about the many ways we can meet your current requirements with the quality and service you have expected of us over the years.

We value our longstanding relationship and look forward to seeing you again in the near future.

Sincerely,

XYZ Corporation

If you have made specific changes such as closing an office or discontinuing a product line, this letter is where you will discuss this fact, explaining the reasons for your move with a positive thrust. Make your letter welcoming and, for those who may have been concerned about your stability, reassuring as well.

HOW TO RELAUNCH YOUR BUSINESS WITH A NEW LOOK AND A NEW ATTITUDE

After you have let everyone know that you're still in business, you want to make a real splash to develop the thrust to take your company to the next level of progress. The most notorious and successful campaign such as this was one employed by Chrysler after a long period where its survival was called into question and it required the federal government to guarantee its loans.

Under the successful leadership of Lee Iaccoca, the company completed a successful reorganization and announced it with a major promotion of "The New Chrysler Corporation." It was an advertising campaign that firmly left the impression in the eyes of the car-buying public that this was a company that was back in the market big time and for the long haul. This is important to a car buyer because they are concerned about the long-term service of their vehicles. You may think that Continental Airlines would come out of its *second* Chapter 11 bankruptcy quietly, but that's not what it did. After its plan was approved, Continental took out full-page ads in major papers, including *USA Today,* to announce the fact. The traveling public wants to be sure that their airline ticket will be usable when they need it, and Continental made that fact loud and clear.

If you can find a cost-effective way to create a new image for your company by changing your logo or even your name, you should consider it. Now is the time to raise your profile, not lower it. Take advantage of every public relation opportunity that is offered to make your presence felt. Donate prizes to a charity event, sponsor a summer youth team who will wear the name of your company, take a booth at a trade fair, or begin to advertise aggressively.

If you can stage a large promotion or sales event, that may be the way to relaunch your company. If you have opened a new store or freshened up your existing place of business, how about holding an open house? Even if you have moved into small or more efficient quarters to save money, make it into a positive. Do everything you can to bring your company and your capabilities to the attention of existing as well as potential customers. After all, this is the reason you went into business in the first place!

HOW TO CHECK THE PULSE OF YOUR BUSINESS

You must learn to step back periodically and take an overall review and overview of your operation. You can schedule a visit with your accountant to discuss your results and go over future plans. You may want to go away for the day with your staff and have an open discussion about the progress of the business and share new ideas and strategies.

Continue the exercise of spreading year-to-year results by actual numbers as well as percentages side by side to see if there have been any changes, positive or negative. Compare your own results to the industry averages, and make sure you are keeping pace.

I have filled hundreds of pages with advice and examples of how a turnaround works and how you can keep your business in good health. Before I come to the end of this chapter, I would like to add the advice of someone else. It is good advice because, like mine, it was learned in the trenches. Some believe that is the only way to really find out about the facts of business life.

The man I am about to quote is named Dan Goetz, and he is the chairman of Stylette, a manufacturing company that is a division of a billion-dollar corporation. In his 30-year-plus career in business Dan has started three companies and turned around more than a few more. Dan is also currently the acting chairman of the board of a small Pittsburgh bank. He has quite a lot of wisdom about business that he is often asked to share. Three pieces of his advice resonated to me, and they are

1. Find out where the information is buried.
2. Always listen to the winds of change.
3. Set your priorities in terms of the probable not the possible.

I shall always keep these in mind, and I suggest you do the same.

SUMMING UP

This chapter of your business life is about to end, and a new phase will begin. The first day is today and there are a few things to accomplish to assure that the future will begin and continue on an even keel. The following are some points to remember:

1. You need to accomplish a conclusion to your turnaround.
2. You should deliver a copy of your new business plan to your banker and your professional advisors.
3. You should meet with your employees to acknowledge their efforts and inform them of your intentions for the future.
4. Vendors and customers need to be kept informed.

5. Be proud of your accomplishment and create a high profile.
6. Keep active in the market—promote—promote—promote.
7. Don't allow yourself to get so caught up in the day-to-day fire-fighting that you lose your sense of overview.
8. Be optimistic—the best years are ahead.
9. Be realistic—there are always mine fields to avoid.
10. Be kind to yourself—you are an important asset to everyone around you.

PART FIVE

How a Small Retail Operation Turned Its Business Around

Ray and Mary Ann Carr (not their real names) have operated a business together for most of their 12 years of marriage. Ray's family had been in the retail business for 40 years, and Ray started his own business with one neighborhood shoe store. Ray did most of the buying, and his store carried a very basic line of women's shoes with a much more limited selection of men's shoes. In the early years, the store carried no children's shoes. Mary Ann's work at the store involved selling two days a week and doing most of the bookkeeping at home. An accountant prepared statements every six months and took care of the Carr's tax returns. They made a comfortable income for their long hours and a medium amount of stress.

After five years, Ray was offered a favorable lease on a second location, and together the Carrs decided it was a solid opportunity. The same line of shoes would be sold in the new store, although for the past year, this had also included a line of athletic shoes for men, women, and teenagers that had proven to be very profitable. It was those extra profits that were used to open the second store, which was operating at a profit by the third month. Two good years in two stores followed.

The third store came along after a slightly down year, and perhaps that precipitated the risk of expansion. Profits were off, and like many retailers, the Carrs looked to the nearby shopping mall as the source of their problem as well as the ultimate solution. A new strip mall was about to open, and even though rents were 50 percent higher than the other two stores, Ray believed this was a solid move. The developer required a five-year lease and added the cost of the build-outs to the rent.

The work required in a third store opening took more time than Ray or Mary Ann had anticipated. They could barely keep up the pace and were neglecting to pay the same amount of attention to the existing stores that had contributed to their previous success. The original stores were operating only marginally, and unsold inventory was building, primarily in the high-priced athletic shoes where sales remained flat.

The mall store proved to be far more expensive to operate than the Carrs had projected—they were open 11 hours a day for six days a week and 6 hours a day the seventh for a total of 72 hours. Hiring staff to cover the hours adequately raised the overhead to twice what it was in the other stores, and the mall opened slowly with the rest of the new stores delayed. Early revenues came in at 20 percent of projections. It was a disaster from day 1. The other stores moving in were more high scale than the basic footwear the Carrs carried, and they weren't benefiting from the typical mall traffic. In a panic after six months of losses that put the three stores into the red, the Carrs tried to find a more expensive line of footwear to generate increased sales in store 3. One of the major manufacturers required a large initial purchase and 50 percent of the invoice in advance. The Carrs came up with the money, but only with the use of a bank line of credit that had seldom been used before this crisis. A few months later with the new store still not performing and draining resources from the other two, the credit line was being used to meet current expenses. This small retail operation was on its way to extinction. Physically exhausted and emotionally drained, the Carrs went to a lawyer to discuss their options—they were convinced that they were on their way to bankruptcy. And if they hadn't taken strong and quick action, they would have been.

PHASE ONE— TAKING STEPS TO STABILIZE THE SITUATION

When I first met the Carrs, the stress of their situation was evidenced by both their own description of their feelings and the fact that they weren't doing anything because they were completely unsure of where to start. This immobilization is often the biggest hurdle an entrepreneur faces and can be the primary reason to bring in an outsider to get the ball rolling.

Bank balances were precariously low and the first task was to build them up. I advised against Ray and Mary Ann borrowing against personal assets to put in extra capital. While this may have been an option down the road, now was too soon to risk their personal finances as well.

Since the company had always done well in the past, and Mary Ann had been diligent about paying bills on time, all her overhead payables were current. Cash flow was instantaneous because all the sales were cash, check, or credit card. Difficult as it was for the Carrs, we stopped making any payments for 20 days and harvested all the cash as a cushion. Knowing that she could pay bills if she had to helped to calm Mary Ann's concerns.

Vendors were a different issue. A number of them were already demanding money, so that's where I stepped in. I called each one of them and introduced myself as a consultant who was working with the Carrs to restructure their finances. I asked for a moratorium on payments for 30 days, and all but one supplier agreed. He made noises as if he was going to go to court to force payment, and we decided that we didn't have the money to fight him off at the moment. I promised to check back in ten days, and he stopped threatening legal actions for the moment.

Next we planned to raise extra money through a special sale, particularly of the high-priced merchandise in the new store that hadn't been selling. We wanted promotion for the sale but didn't want to spend any of our precious cash. We found a graphic artist willing to do a sale flyer for store credit in lieu of money. We would have been willing to offer this same barter deal to other creditors if we could have found anyone interested.

Our next step was to deal with the overhead issues of the new location that we all believed were the most serious problem facing the business (later on we were in for a surprise). The agent who managed the new mall was very sympathetic with our predicament. He still had some stores unoccupied and the last thing he wanted was for a store less than a year old to go under. We came away from that meeting with more than we hoped—one month free rent and 50 percent off on a second month's rent. This was meant to help us get back on our feet and be able to fulfill the final years of our lease. Now we had some breathing space!

Several vehicles had been leased to the company for use by the owners as well as one manager to run back and forth between the stores, sometimes exchanging stock. Instead of a panel truck, however, the stores leased a fancy passenger van, a station wagon, and a luxury sedan. The lease on the van was expiring and we decided to turn it in and replace it with a small used truck, which we bought outright. The monthly savings was one $349 payment and almost $1,000 of annual insurance premium.

Next came personnel costs, which proved to be complicated because we had three full-time and two part-time workers at our troubled store to keep it covered sufficiently. We cut back two people but ended up hiring one back for fewer hours.

The Carrs took a 30 percent pay cut, but we all agreed that this would be for 90 days and then we would review the situation. The cash crunch had ended, and operations were no longer at a loss. But the solutions were temporary.

The "we" involved were both of the Carrs and the attorney who brought me together with them, the new store manager who was Ray's cousin, and another store owner in the mall who was concerned about our business setting a precedent for the new center. The other store owner was very helpful about traffic and demographic trends of the shopping area, something that hadn't been considered before the store opening; he didn't attend all our strategy sessions, but he was helpful when he was available.

The one missing link was an accountant, as the one the Carrs had been using was little more than a bookkeeper—he took records and put them into monthly statements, but never gave any advice, good, bad, or indifferent. Even when profits were going down in the two store operations, no warning was ever sounded. It could have been a fatal mistake. We knew we had to find a new accountant, and we started looking.

Our cash flow was better, and the Carrs started to sleep better and breathe easier. Their family relationships were strong, and it was clear that they were a source of comfort to each other. I have seen many entrepreneurs facing business difficulties isolate themselves from their friends and families at a time when they need them the most. We discussed the issue but didn't feel the need to dwell on it.

The Carrs and I, along with the company attorney, discussed the possibility of a Chapter 11 bankruptcy reorganization. The maxed-out line of credit was less than $70,000, and it was totally secured by inventory. If we disposed of unsecured debt and canceled the mall lease, the balance sheet started to look pretty good. Ray and Mary Ann both were disturbed by the idea and I sympathized with that attitude. In a dire emergency, bankruptcy is an option, but few business owners want to make this difficult decision.

We also considered an unforced liquidation sale: the ultimate closing of the business or a sale of all three stores, which included all assets and at least would have continued the business with new owners. These options were preferable, but both owners, now more relaxed, were committed to a turnaround.

We also considered the possibility that some aggressive marketing would improve sales at the dreaded third store and that the whole small chain would operate once again at a profit. We brainstormed ideas of low-cost promotions and reviewed ways to create increased traffic along with other tenants at the mall. At the same time we brainstormed ideas about the two original stores. We didn't want to get so bogged down in our struggle that we didn't see the bright spots and capitalize on them.

For the first two weeks, we met every other day, and then we met twice a week, although we had phone conferences in between. The first month was very intense, but we all felt as if we made progress by the end of it. The immediate crisis had passed—longer-term problems needed to be solved.

PHASE TWO— CONDUCTING AN IN-DEPTH ANALYSIS OF THE BUSINESS

We uncovered some very surprising results once we set about taking a hard look at every different aspect of the operation. We all had assumed that the main problem was the cost of the mall store and the lack of vibrant sales. Since all the monthly statements had shown the consolidated results of all three stores, part of the real story was buried in the books.

By this time we had a new accountant, and while she was getting up to speed, we all decided that we had to conduct a store-by-store analysis. The mall store was operating at a loss—this wasn't a surprise—but what did get our attention was that the loss was smaller than we expected. Equally unanticipated were the even larger losses at the other two stores. Now we had to dig deeper to find out how the entire operation had deteriorated from its profitable days. This required a complete inventory analysis showing what level of unsold products we had in every line. Over the past three or four months, a lot of inventory was moved from store to store—we could not afford to be very deep in most sizes and styles except the most popular movers, so when stock got low, shoes were transferred. No one really knew what inventory was where anymore.

When the numbers came in, the story was clear. The same athletic shoes that had made so much profit over the years were now a millstone around the company's neck. Unsold shoes, some odd sizes and some just not "this year's" model, were abundant. Profits on the shoes sold were virtually wiped out by leftover inventory. On the one hand, it was good to have some answers, but the down side was it made us wonder if there were any good sales left in the company. Most of this information would have been available if we had installed good point-of-sale software in each store. Instead, we had to reconstruct information comparing purchase records to sales records to inventory records. It was a complicated process, but even so, the information we wanted was available. Had we not committed to an in-depth analysis, the Carrs might never have determined where their most serious problems originated. Early on, we all believed that if we closed the expensive location, the profit drain would be stopped.

Now that we knew what was wrong, we wanted to take a look at what we did well so that we could begin to rebuild on those strengths. Once we had isolated the losses suffered on our sports line shoes, the real profitability of our original core line of shoes became evident. The gross revenue of these products had remained flat, but I suspected that it was due to the fact that more of the floor space of the store had been given over to the athletic shoe line. Early in their business, the Carrs had carried every shoe in the line of their major supplier, but now they displayed about 60 percent of the line. If we restated our results based on the margins of our basic line and not the combination with our less profitable athletic shoes, these stores would have all operated in the black. That gave us all real hope for the future of this business.

At the end of this phase, I requested a meeting entirely dedicated to soul searching. Our work was only half done, and I wanted to make sure we moved forward in the direction that the Carrs wanted to go. At one point, they both mentioned a desire to give it all up and move to a warmer climate. We didn't take the comments seriously, though, because most Pittsburghers say that at least once halfway through the winter.

Now, however, was the time to have an open discussion about what the Carrs really wanted over the next five or ten years. We could have closed the stores or sold the chain or considered any number of strategies. What was decided by this meeting was that Ray and Mary Ann wanted to stay in business if it could be made more manageable. They were both completely worn out by the stress of the last year and now admitted that they had been feeling overwhelmed before the deal on the mall location had been completed but both of them were reluctant to admit that fact to the other. Now that we had these facts out in the open, we could all agree on what we wanted to accomplish. Even if we could turn the third store into a profitable location, this was one too many and it had to be closed. Both Ray and Mary Ann were relieved by our meeting and both felt that they could hang on long enough to get their lives back in order.

PHASE THREE— RESTRUCTURING THE BUSINESS

The Carrs, their attorney, and I spent many hours considering what our strategy would be. We had three leases to consider, and the one we really wanted out of was a five-year term with almost four years remaining on it. The mall wasn't completely full yet, and we didn't think the landlord would allow us out without a penalty. With the current debt burden, this would have been impossible.

Our vendor credit was also at its limit, and we needed to liquidate inventory to pay old bills. At the same time we had to make the decision about any product line changes we wanted to put into place so that inventory could be ordered. We made the decision to deemphasize the sports shoes and go back to our basic good-quality–good-value lines. We still had loyal customers for those products, and we felt they would continue to trade with us. We knew where we wanted to go; the question then was how to get there. This was the plan:

1. Put the athletic shoes in a special sale section of each store and discount them deeply to liquidate.
2. Bring in new merchandise for the two original locations and promote this fact.
3. Begin to negotiate a deal with the mall store—our rent was less than rents now being charged, and we had a number of fixtures and improvements we had done that could be included. We hoped to sublet the space.
4. Negotiate a payout with suppliers on old bills while paying new invoices in terms.

The outcome of this plan was mixed, but in the end it exceeded our expectations.

1. The shoe liquidation went very slowly. New improvements had been made to many of the walking and jogging shoe lines that made our shoes obsolete. We kept cutting prices until we found the point where they would move. It was less than cost, but it was cash.
2. The new merchandise was ordered a bit late, and not all that we wanted came in, but the reemphasis of this is the stores immediately increased in traffic and sales. Old customers came back more frequently to find out what we had gotten in stock. The Carrs said it was beginning to feel like the old days.
3. This is where we really succeeded. Someone approached Ray about the mall because they were considering opening up a store selling shoes with a much higher price level than ours. This prospect wanted to know about the management of the mall and how traffic had been over the first year of operation. In the end, he took over the Carrs's lease, paid them for the assignment because he was saving over $20,000 from a new lease, bought all the fixtures and shelving, and so on. The landlord agreed to this because he felt his cooperation would be good public relations.

4. All the vendors eventually came around and made the deal we wanted. Old bills would be cleaned up in a year, and no new ones would get to be past due. The Carrs lived up to their promises.

Lest you think that this whole episode was easy to end, let me assure you that was not the case. There was still a maxed-out line of credit with the bank, and now that there was one less store and far less inventory on our books, the bank grew a bit difficult. Initially, the banker wanted us to reduce the line by a substantial amount, which would have been impossible. For a while he wouldn't give in at all, and we thought after all our good work, there might still be a bankruptcy ahead to force a solution. In the end, however, we were able to term out the loan over a period of years with the SBA guaranteeing 70 percent of the loan. The procedures for these types of loans have been streamlined over the past few years and our approval took less than 30 days. We all breathed a collective sigh of relief.

At this point, our new accountant made herself known by two important discoveries. She had been working on the company's internal record keeping to help us complete our profit analysis, and her investigation led the Carrs to discover that their income had been overstated for two years. New tax returns were prepared, and a refund was forthcoming in excess of $5,000. Not only did we have a small fund of capital, but our accountant knew exactly what to do with it. A new computerized point-of-sale register was ordered for both stores immediately on a lease–purchase agreement, and it was installed in less than two weeks. The two remaining stores were almost running themselves, and they were both operating at a profit.

The process had taken almost eight months to complete, although there were times when we worked relentlessly to beat a deadline or solve a pressing problem and others when weeks passed uneventfully. We all agreed that we needed a short break before we tackled some loose ends and created a plan for the future.

By the end of this third phase, the Carrs had spent almost $18,000 in fees to attorney, accountant, and consultant although some of this would have been spent normally. We generated excess cash well above the fees with inventory liquidation, the sale of the mall lease and equipment, and the tax refund. Serious and growing losses were turned into profits. This was a cost-effective venture made even more so by the Carrs's very conservative use of professionals. They completed many of the tasks themselves initially to save money, but in the end, they acknowledged that this had been a learning experience as well.

PHASE FOUR—FUTURE PLANS

Our short break turned into six weeks, and even after that length of time, we canceled a few meetings before finally getting together. With no pressing problems, we all felt casual about the next phase of our work. Once we were together again exchanging our old "war" stories, the sense of urgency increased. We realized that after such a stressful experience, no one wanted to take the risk of anything jeopardizing our recovery.

First on our agenda was a new marketing strategy to create greater revenue from the two remaining stores. We wanted to increase our number of products so that we could maximize our sales per square foot. A jewelry designer had approached the Carrs about selling her designs at one of their stores. Mary Ann met with her and came back to report that the work was unique and priced competitively for originals. There was enough quantity to be able to sell at both stores, and the Carrs made a consignment deal with the designer. Each time a piece was sold, the Carrs took 40 percent of the sales price and sent the balance to the designer. This was a successful start, but it was only a start.

Once most of the athletic shoes were sold off, there was even more excess space in each store to fill, and then the real planning began. Ray wanted to expand the line of children's shoes, and Mary Ann thought they should look for other consignment products and not take any new purchasing risks. She won the argument temporarily—we all agreed to aggressively change the look of one store, and if it worked, the second store would follow suit.

Mary Ann set out to find new products and found a line of good-quality purses and some interesting leather jackets as well. Both manufacturers would only sell outright, but the inventory requirements wouldn't be impossible because sizes were limited on the garments and nonexistent on the purses. The look of the store was changed to feature the new complete line of accessories and sales went up by 25 percent almost immediately. We tempered our enthusiasm because we knew this was the draw of something new and wouldn't sustain at this level, but we expected long-term gains in excess of 10 percent. Based on the experience, the second store was also changed, and the new lines added there also.

These moves had the best possible effect on the Carrs and their employees. With all their time and energy being invested in projects for the future, the past seemed even more distant. Certainly, the tension was gone and everyone seemed more energized. Now was the time to tap into that energy to create additional marketing plans and get everyone behind these efforts.

About the time the second store was upgraded, one of the local store owners suggested a joint promotion by all the local merchants. The Carrs were in a perfect mode for projects such as this, and Ray became active in the committee. The results of the three-day sale were very good.

My work was coming to an end, and the last goal I wanted the Carrs to accomplish was to write a business plan. Ray wasn't interested in the task, so Mary Ann and I decided to do the work and then show it to him. We went through all the steps until we came to the section about future potential and the company's plans. Putting it all in writing made Mary Ann consider the fact that there would be a number of changes facing them over the next 20 plus years of their work life. She decided that it was important to take a review every few years to consider their overall progress and plan for the next few years on almost all the aspects of the operations of the stores. Neighborhoods change, and along with that, the types of customers change. At times, even the suppliers change—one had closed and an entire line was discontinued over the year we had been working together.

The three-year pro forma statement was encouraging. If progress was steady and no unexpected disaster hit, the Carrs could return to a comfortable income with medium levels of stress. That's all they ever wanted.

The experience of a near disaster had a profound effect on the Carrs—it was interesting that they saw the changes as being a positive force. Their lives were more focused, and they had a greater appreciation of the good times. It's a result I've seen before, including in myself. This is a bonus for all the stress and hard work. And, finally, the Carrs felt well prepared to face whatever challenges lay ahead.

PART SIX

From the Professionals

Answers to Most Frequently Asked Questions

FROM THE ACCOUNTANT— ISRAEL RUDOY, CPA

Israel Rudoy is the managing partner of Horowitz, Rudoy & Roteman, a Pittsburgh accounting firm providing a wide variety of services, including accounting, auditing, business evaluation, and tax planning. Mr. Rudoy's interest in the welfare of his business clients is evident from a single meeting with him. This size and type firm is a valuable asset to any entrepreneur.

Q. What kind of financial information should I be getting and from whom?

A. A business owner should see a minimum of monthly financial statements that can be drawn internally. There are a number of software systems available to provide this information, and they are readily available, easy to use, and low in cost. You should also see a monthly aging of your accounts receivable and accounts payable.

On a quarterly basis, you should review an inventory figure that has been maintained on a running system or taken physically. Always take a look at the method used to cost the inventory and consider how salable your inventory really is in today's terms.

Q. How often should I see my accountant?

A. It depends on the quality of your internal information. Your accountant can review your documents periodically.

At a minimum, you should meet with an accountant three times a year as follows:

- After the first 6 months to review how you are doing.
- After 11 months to plan for taxes *before* the end of the year.
- After 12 months to close your year.

Q. What is cash flow?

A. The dollars generated by a business after all expenses and debt payment. This is your net cash retained without consideration of noncash adjustments such as depreciation.

Q. How can I tell how much my company is worth?

A. Owners typically cannot do their own calculation. You should have an evaluation done by an independent business appraiser. Some of the considerations would be the following:

- How your results compare to industry averages.
- A review of several years' income statements.
- A review of hard assets.
- An evaluation of intangible assets such as good will and market share.

The market value of a going concern is the value established between two interested parties. In other words, the worth of your company can have a range depending on the type of buyer and timing of the sale.

Q. What is meant by the "book value" of my equipment?

A. The historical cost less the accumulated depreciation that results in an estimated value.

The going-concern value of equipment would be higher and the liquidated value of equipment would normally be lower, especially if it were a forced sale.

Book value is often a fair estimate between the two.

Q. Should my accountant go with me to the bank?

A. Yes—it can really help. Many entrepreneurs don't know how to talk to their bankers. They are good salesmen but not familiar with the fundamentals. That's where an accountant can be of real help.

Q. What do you put in a loan package?

A. At least three years of statements.

- Financial projections for the period of the loan—quarterly for most bankers but monthly for the SBA. The calculations are meant to show how you are going to pay back the loan.
- A statement concerning the purpose of the loan.
- Any pertinent business information such as catalogs, technical information or copies of new contracts.

Q. I can't pay the bank. What should I do?

A. Call your banker immediately—if you wait until he calls you, the situation will already have deteriorated and you will have fewer options.

Q. I can't pay my taxes. What should I do?

A. Always *file* the return even if you can't pay.

We are currently in a "good feeling" era with the IRS, and they are being directed to allow for most reasonable payment plans. Offer the best payment terms you can, and they will let you know if that is acceptable.

Mr. Rudoy's good advice:

- It is critical for entrepreneurs to have someone they respect who can tell them they're wrong.
- Never, never owe the IRS.
- You should know when to get out.

FROM THE ATTORNEY— DONALD L. PHILLIPS

Don Phillips is the senior partner of Phillips & Galanter, a small commercial law firm in Pittsburgh. His practice over the past 30-plus years has concentrated on debtors' and creditors' rights.

Q. How can I collect what is owed to me?

A. There are a number of things to consider in the area of bill collecting.

- Have a good internal receivable process. Watch all new customers and make calls immediately when payment is late.
- Understand the standards for your industry—is there dating? Are most bills paid in 60 days or after the season? Determine when the bill is absolutely due.
- Find the debtor's "threshold of payment." For some it is constant phone calls or reminder stickers. Some require certified letters or threats of a lawsuit.

- Determine when the person who is paying you was paid for the goods or the job. If he hasn't paid you by then, he's probably using your money and you may not get paid.
- Don't give up a percentage of your claim (to a collector) unless there is a good reason.

Q. When should I turn an account over for collection?

A. An account that is turned over is done so for salvage, not for collection. Most agencies are successful on about 30 percent of their cases, and lawyers have about the same rate of success.

Agencies will charge you on the average 20 percent of what they collect. Attorneys will charge a fee of 25–35 percent plus any court costs.

With these odds, you may not net anywhere near the amount you anticipate by turning over the account for collection. Do so if your debtor is actively evading any of your contacts.

Q. My creditors are threatening to sue. What should I do?

A. Pay some money on account. You know that they will lose at least 25 percent of the debt by taking legal action, and, it is hoped, they take that into consideration when deciding what action to pursue.

If your creditors accept partial payment, that does not mean that they have agreed to accept this form of payout. However, if you make this type of offer verbally, confirm it in writing when you send your check. At least, you will have some defense to any legal action that may be instigated.

If the debt is yours, you will have to pay it eventually. Do what you can to avoid a judgment.

Q. One of my creditors has taken a judgment against my company. What happens next?

A. A judgment will allow your creditor to cause an execution of that judgment by a sheriff. This enforcement can attach your bank account, levy on your car or other vehicle, or even the contents of your cash register. Your creditor can serve attachments on people who owe you money.

There are some legal actions you can take to reopen a judgment, but the only way to undo this action is by a bankruptcy petition.

Q. I'm behind in my rent. Can my landlord lock me out of my building?

A. Yes; this is legal self-help that is available to landlords. In most cases, they cannot sell your belongings without notice and some type of court action. The only way to undo this action is also by a bankruptcy filing.

Q. If I've signed a contract for products that I can no longer afford, what can I do?

A. A contract would be binding regardless of the change in your circumstance. But your supplier would not want to ship goods and not get paid. Try to negotiate a settlement.

If the supplier can mitigate his damages by selling the goods elsewhere, it would make sense for him to do so and you may be held liable only for the difference in selling price.

You do have legal responsibility for any and all contracts you sign.

Mr. Phillips's good advice:

- Don't borrow from taxing authorities; your debt will grow quickly and you may be violating criminal laws.
- Communication with a little bit of money can have a very strong effect.

FROM THE BANKER—THOMAS NUNNALLY

Tom Nunnally has been a banker for 25 years, 20 of them in Pittsburgh. He is currently a vice-president of North Side Deposit Bank and a full-time small business enthusiast. He prefaced his answers by saying that he wished his customers would ask more questions.

Q. How can the bank help my company without making any new loans?

A. The amount of help a banker can give is often determined by your past relationship with the bank. If you have been in previous difficulty, your loans may already be classified as "substandard, doubtful or less." You don't want to be on this list because this fact will limit the authority of your local banker.

In most cases, your banker can temporarily defer or modify payments on a term loan. Principal payments can be deferred for a number of months and interest-only payments be required.

A banker can also help in finding supplemental financing through a number of government agencies including the SBA. For a single large order, special contract financing is possible.

Q. If I show progress in a turnaround, how much of an improvement do I have to make before I can get additional financing?

A. It all depends on how well you can show the ability to pay. If you have made a substantial cut in costs or received a new contract, these factors will be taken into consideration. It may take as little as three months.

Any loan proposal should also give any of the alternatives that you have considered if your progress doesn't continue. Show that you have a contingency plan.

Q. How often should I submit information to the bank and in what form?

A. This depends on the size of the bank; the bigger the bank, the more information they require.

You should submit the following on a quarterly basis:

- Company-prepared profit and loss statement—signed by an officer and dated.
- Summary of assets—receivables aging.
- Summary of inventory.
- Payables aging by amount not individual account.

On an annual basis, you should submit an accountant-prepared financial statement and a personal statement.

Q. Would the bank release its lien on my excess equipment so that I can sell it?

A. For most bankers, the issue is where the money will be used. It is less likely if the use is for paying off old bills.

It is more likely if the money is meant to fund a new project.

You may offer to use part of the proceeds to reduce your bank debt, and if your loan is still well secured, you may get cooperation.

Q. Could the bank use my personal assets as security for a new loan?

A. Yes, in fact, to many bankers, this is a good sign of owner determination. If you believe in your effort to turn things around, your bank is more likely to believe in your effort.

Q. Why can't I get a verbal commitment for a loan before I make formal application?

A. Your banker is constrained on two fronts.

1. Federal government regulators have requirements regarding record keeping and equal credit laws that limit most banks from making decisions without a complete set of paperwork.
2. Concern over litigation makes most bankers reticent to give any verbal assurances before all information has been received. If a rejection is made based on unknown or undisclosed liens or judgments, the banker can be sued over verbal representations. Few bankers will take that risk.

Q. How quickly can I get a loan in case of a serious short-term cash shortage?

A. This would be directly proportionate to your previous relationship with your banker.

- If you have had a successful ongoing relationship, it could be as quickly as overnight.
- It could take up to a week if all checks are required.
- If your account has been classified, quick loan turnarounds are impossible.

Mr. Nunnally's good advice:

- Step back for a while, evaluate where you are, and see if you still have a business. If your target has moved, you must decide whether you can change to meet a new niche.
- Be proactive in your communication.

FROM THE CONSULTANT— SUZANNE CAPLAN

Suzanne Caplan has been a consultant to other small business owners for over 16 years, originally working with start-ups and for the last 2 years concentrating on small business turnarounds.

Q. If I don't need a supplier anymore, do I have to pay him?

A. Yes, although you may make a tougher offer than you would to a necessary vendor.

All creditors, even those you no longer need, can take legal action against you. They can report you to a credit agency or to other suppliers and make your life very difficult.

Always call any creditor and try to work out a deal you can live up to and then settle the debt.

Q. How truthful do I have to be to my banker?

A. If your situation is very bad, chances are your banker already knows. You never want to misrepresent anything to a bank—getting caught will damage your relationship and could be a fraudulent misrepresentation that can be prosecuted criminally.

What you can do is put the emphasis on all your positive information and not discuss any of the problems unless you are asked. Be optimistic in your projections but not unrealistic.

Q. Will the bank take my house?

A. I have never known a banker who really wanted a lender's home, although I have had two clients who actually heard that threat. Your bank is in the business of money, not real estate.

If your loan really goes bad, the bank will write it off. That's why they must maintain a reserve fund. Once it's over 90 days delinquent, your loan is put in a separate category. I have been surprised by some of the settlement offers a bank will accept.

Q. Doesn't the SBA have to lend money to small businesses in trouble?

A. In a word, no. The SBA will make loans that are more questionable than the bank, but they have credit criteria as well.

Most SBA loans are made through a bank with the agency guaranteeing only part of the loan, so the standards of the bank are those that prevail.

Q. Will I ever get credit again?

A. You probably will. In fact, in many cases, the fact that you stayed in business and worked to pay off debts will work in your favor. If you have the sales that your suppliers want, they will be willing to negotiate with you.

Even after coming out of bankruptcy, my company was able to reestablish open credit terms.

Ms. Caplan's good advice:

- Don't bury your head in the sand and hope your troubles will go away. The sooner you face your situation and get good advice, the likelier you are to triumph.

EPILOGUE

If you have finished this book hoping that you would find a magic bullet within its pages, you are out of luck. Just as there were no easy ways to start up and grow your business, the road back from difficulty is long and hazardous. The difference between the early days and now is that you were full of energy and promise then and now you are probably worn down and filled to the brim with frustration.

What I can offer you is hope—for the success you can have turning around your company—and assurance—that it won't last forever. If you follow the program I have outlined, you should begin to see some improvement in less than a month, and in three months, you should be headed back to profitability. The entire program may take you a year, but I know you'll find that once the immediate pressure is relieved, your working life will improve.

I know also that it isn't easy to reach out to family, friends, and associates for the help you want and need. You may be feeling a loss of confidence in your own ability or even anger at what's happening around you. After all, you're honest, you work hard, and at one time you believed that you had a certain amount of ability. If all this is true, then why has your business life become such a nightmare? There isn't one simple explanation for how any business gets into trouble and you need to focus your energy on how you're going to work yourself out. Virtually every small business faces critical problems at least once. The important issue isn't that you hit a wall; rather, it's how you come off that wall.

Many successful careers have been built out of ashes—in fact, it is commonly believed that you learn from your failures, not from your successes. I know you will come out of this experience with great savvy and insight. I know because I have been there, and I've seen this phenomenon in most of my clients. The inner strength they develop along the way is inspiring.

As I was completing this book, a story ran in *The Wall Street Journal* about William Bennett, the chairman of Circus, Circus Enterprises, Inc. Now 69, Bennett is estimated to be worth over $600 million. In 1965, after selling a small business empire experiencing trouble, Bennett had filed for personal bankruptcy. At 41, he started over again. This is a story you will see time and time again if you watch for it.

I'm not saying you'll be a millionaire once this phase of your business life is over. What I am saying is that this is only a phase in your life, and it will not stop you from doing or being anything you are capable of and motivated to accomplish. Believe this and it will be your truth.

It takes courage to take new risks on top of ones that haven't worked out as you expected. I respect you for making the decision to continue the life of a business perhaps you founded and one you still believe in. If you would like to tell me how your effort has succeeded, I would like to hear from you. You may contact me at the following address:

Suzanne Caplan
Suite 212
2927 West Liberty Avenue
Pittsburgh, Pennsylvania 15216

RESOURCE GUIDE

BOOKS

General Information

Applegate, Jane, *Succeeding in Small Business,* Plume (1992). This is a book structured around 101 questions that many entrepreneurs face at one time or another in their business lives.

Clark, Scott, *Beating the Odds: 10 Smart Steps to Small Business Success,* AMACOM (1991). A step-by-step how-to-succeed for the small business owner.

Hawken, Paul, *Growing a Business,* Fireside Books (1988). This is one of the classic books about entrepreneurship. It gives a good philosophical insight into what it means to be in business.

Kirk, Randy W., *When Friday Isn't Payday: A Complete Guide to Starting, Running—and Surviving in—a Very Small Business,* Warner Books (1993). Solid and practical advice from an author who has been there, including advice on how to deal with some thorny temporary crises.

Merrill, Ronald E., and Henry Sedgwich, *The New Venture Handbook—Everything You Need to Know to Start and Run Your Own Business—Revised,* AMACOM (1993). Sophisticated yet practical—this book may help business owners identify the land mines before they step on them.

Prentice Hall Small Business Survival Guide, Prentice Hall Editorial Staff (1993). Strategies of sales and marketing from hiring a sales force through credit and collection.

Rice, Craig S., *Strategic Planning for the Small Business,* Bob Adams (1990). How to evaluate, set objectives, test, and analyze. This book will help to increase your strategic thinking.

Rye, David E., *The Vest-Pocket Entrepreneur,* Prentice Hall (1995). (Soon to be published)

Smith, Brian R., *How to Become Successfully Self-employed,* Bob Adams (1993).

Williams, Bruce, *In Business for Yourself,* Scarborough House (1991). This is a very complete small business primer covering a wide variety of issues. Williams has been there and his advice is easy to follow and sensible.

Sales and Marketing Information

Fournies, Ferdinand F., *Why Customers Don't Do What You Want Them to Do—And What to Do About It,* McGraw Hill (1994). How to understand the psyche of your customer and how to get him to do what serves both of you the best.

Levinson, Jay Conrad, *Guerrilla Marketing,* Houghton Mifflin (1984). A real small business classic. How to develop a lively marketing program with your time and effort in place of big money.

Financial Information

Bergeth, Robert L., *12 Secrets to Cashing Out—How to Sell Your Company for the Most Profit,* Prentice Hall (1994). A practical guide on how to prepare your business for a sale, where to find a likely buyer, how to set a value, and how to negotiate and close a deal.

Milling, Bryan E., *Cash Flow Problem Solver,* Sourcebooks Trade (1992). A highly technical book, but for anyone able to use the system, it works.

O'Hara, Patrick D., *How to Computerize Your Small Business,* John Wiley (1993).

Seglin, Jeffrey L., *Financing Your Small Business,* McGraw Hill (1990). Traditional as well as more obscure places to find money for a small business.

Silver, A. David, *Cash In on Cash Flow, 50 Tough as Nails Ideas for Revitalizing Your Business,* AMACOM (1993). How to squeeze every dollar from a business operation.

Bankruptcy

Caplan, Suzanne, *Saving Your Business—How to Survive Chapter 11 Bankruptcy and Successfully Reorganize Your Business,* Prentice Hall (1993). The book is a guide to the strategy involved in reorganization that, used along with good legal advice will substantially increase the odds of a successful outcome.

Summers, Mark S., *Bankruptcy Explained—A Guide for Business,* John Wiley (1989). Details of the basics of bankruptcy proceedings not the strategies.

PERIODICALS

Inc. Magazine
P.O. Box 54129
Boulder, Colorado 80322
(800) 234-0999

This magazine is directed at the small business community. Features include company profiles and a practical "Hands On" department with technology sections and a reader response column. Of special interest also is a monthly "Business for Sale" column, which provides the reader with information on how a business is priced and marketed.

Small Business Reports
P.O. Box 53140
Boulder, Colorado 80322
(800) 234-1094

This is a monthly publication that runs long and complete hands-on articles about small business topics such as legal considerations, managing employees, and sales strategies. Each issue also includes a book digest.

ORGANIZATIONS

American Management Association
135 West 50th Street
New York, New York 10020
(212) 903-7915

Offers seminars that are applicable to small and midsize companies.

American Women's Economic Development Corporation
60 East 42nd Street
New York, New York 10165
(800) 222-AWED

This group offers training, assistance, and one-on-one consultation for women business owners.

Center for Entrepreneurial Management, Inc.
180 Varick Street
New York, New York 10014
(212) 633-0060

Sponsors a number of small business courses and seminars.

National Association of Small Business Investment Companies
Suite 200
1199 N. Fairfax Street
Alexandria, Virginia 22314
(703) 683-1601

"Venture Capital—Where to Find It?" which lists 160 small business investment companies nationwide is available from this association for $10.

GOVERNMENT AGENCIES

National Technology Transfer Center
316 Washington Avenue
Wheeling, West Virginia 26003
(304) 243-2455
(800) 678-NTTC

This organization could be a real bonanza to any small business able to capitalize on the collaboration with federal laboratories and their developing technology.

Small Business Administration
1441 L Street
Washington, DC 20416
(202) 606-4000
Answer Desk (800) 827-5722

The 800 number is an electronically operated series of prerecorded messages about a wide variety of small business topics, including financing. During normal business hours, counselors are available on request.

INDEX

D

E

F

G